insight text guide

Victoria Bladen

Henry IV Part I

William Shakespeare

First published in 2011. Reprinted 2012, 2014, 2015, 2016, 2017, 2018, 2019, 2020, 2021, 2022, 2024.

Insight Publications Pty Ltd
3/350 Charman Road
Cheltenham VIC 3192
Australia
Tel: +61 3 8571 4950
Email: books@insightpublications.com.au

www.insightpublications.com.au

National Library of Australia Cataloguing-in-Publication entry:
Bladen, Victoria.
William Shakespeare's Henry IV Part 1: text guide /
Victoria Bladen.
9781921411403 (pbk.)
For secondary school age.
Shakespeare, William, 1564-1616 Shakespeare's
Henry IV, part 1.
Shakespeare, William, 1564-1616–Criticism and
interpretation.
822.33

Other ISBNs:
9781925175752 (digital)

Cover design: The Modern Art Production Group

Printed in Australia by Ligare Book Printers

Author's dedication: This book is dedicated to my brother Simon, with love

contents

CHARACTER MAP

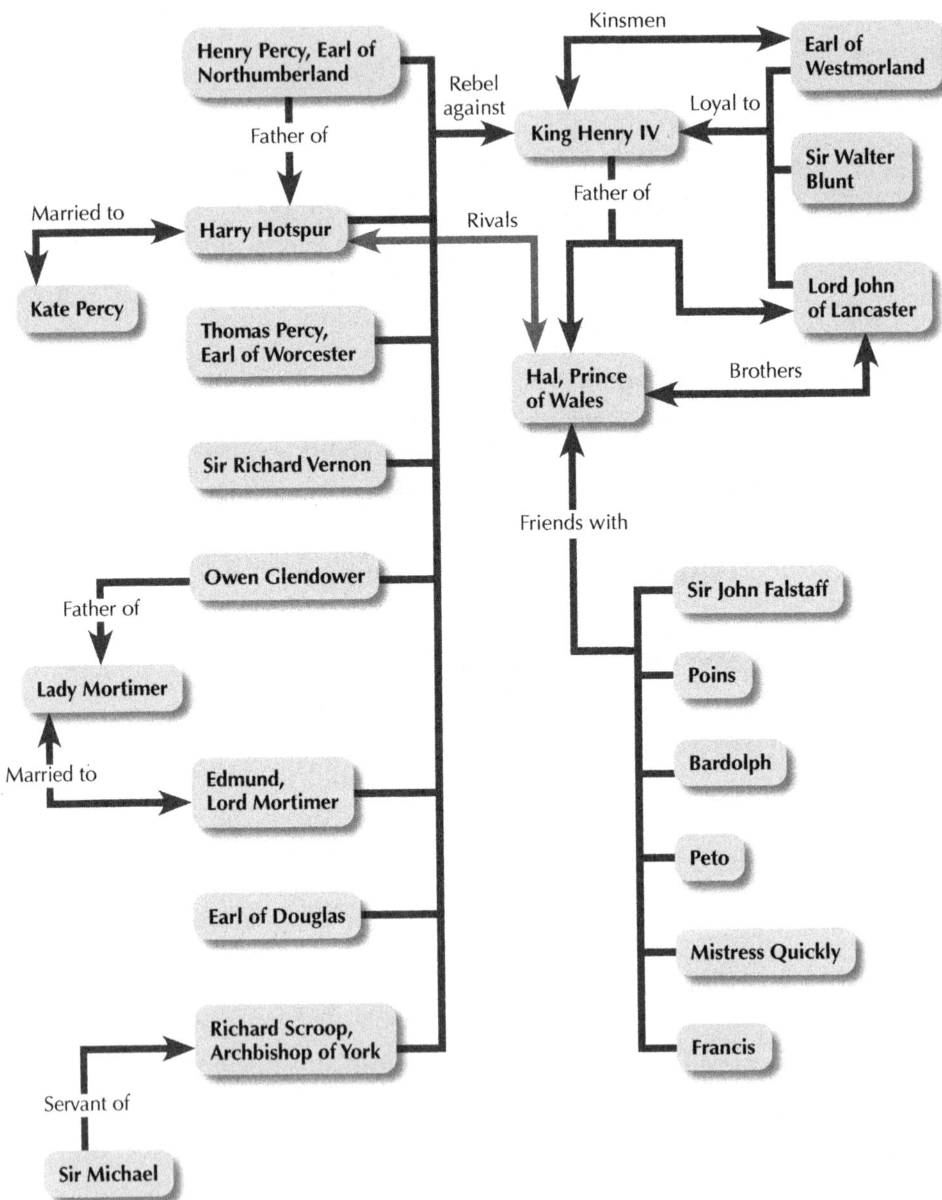

OVERVIEW

William Shakespeare (1564–1616) is one of the most renowned figures of the English literary Renaissance (also referred to as the 'early modern period'). His dramatic and poetic work, written during an intensely productive period from the late sixteenth to the early seventeenth century, has proved capable of enduring well beyond his own time and place. Translated into many languages and adapted for film, television, ballet, opera and graphic novels, Shakespeare's work has evolved into a cultural phenomenon, meaningful and compelling to audiences of different periods and cultures.

1 Henry IV (also commonly referred to as *Henry IV, Part I*) is one of Shakespeare's most popular plays, featuring one of his most beloved characters, Falstaff. This guide is designed to help you navigate your way through the play, organise your thinking and help you to write intelligently and competently about the play in your essays and exams. Remember that *1 Henry IV* is a *play*, created to be experienced as a performance on stage, even though it is often first experienced as a written text or as a film. If you are able to see the play performed you will gain a deeper understanding of its shape, the characters, how the dramatic action unfolds and the effect of Shakespeare's language. Film adaptations will also help you to understand the play, particularly if you are able to view different versions. However, remember that watching a film shouldn't be a substitute for a close reading of the text itself.

About the author

Shakespeare was born in 1564, when Elizabeth I was on the throne, and died in 1616, when James I was king. Born into a middle-class family in Stratford-upon-Avon in Warwickshire, William was the son of John Shakespeare, a glove-maker and landowner, and his wife Mary, a gentleman's daughter. He received an education from the King's New

School in Stratford, but never attended university. As a young man he fell in love with Anne Hathaway, and they were married in 1582 after Anne became pregnant; the child, Susanna, was born six months after the wedding. Twins, Hamnet and Judith, were born in 1585; Hamnet died when he was a child. Subsequently, the marriage seems to have broken down.

In the late 1580s, Shakespeare moved to London and began his career as a playwright. He joined a theatre company called The Lord Chamberlain's Men, which produced plays that were performed at a venue called the Theatre. Shakespeare acted in, wrote plays for and shared in the profits of the theatre company. When the lease over the land on which the Theatre was built expired in 1597, and a dispute with the landlord arose, Shakespeare and his colleagues dismantled the wooden building, took it across the river and reassembled it at Bankside, south of the Thames. This theatre, renamed the Globe, opened in 1599. In London today, a close replica of the Globe stands near the original site, a venue in which Shakespeare's plays are performed all year round.

When James I came to the throne in 1603 he became the patron of the theatre company of which Shakespeare was part owner; the company was therefore renamed the King's Men. The king recognised the huge potential of the theatre to reach many people; in this regard, the theatre can perhaps be thought of as the early seventeenth-century equivalent of television. James wanted his reign to be associated with that 'media' power, despite the fact that in many of Shakespeare's works there is strong criticism of authority figures.

Synopsis

1 Henry IV is about the making of a future king and the qualities a king should have in order to govern well. Should a monarch remain distanced from their subjects or try to understand the ordinary people? The play is also about rebellion and the vulnerability of the crown, a theme continued from Shakespeare's earlier play, *Richard II*. Despite its title, there are several prominent characters in *1 Henry IV* that attract our interest, including the king's son, Prince Hal, who initially wastes his time at the tavern with unruly friends such as Sir John Falstaff, his large comic drinking companion. Another prominent character is Hotspur, a fiery hot-headed rival to Hal and one of a group of rebels from different parts of the kingdom who besiege Henry IV's reign, challenging his right to the crown.

1 Henry IV is the second play in a tetralogy – a group of four plays with interlinked events. (This was the second tetralogy Shakespeare wrote and is often referred to as the *Henriad*.) In the first play, *Richard II*, Henry Bolingbroke deposes the legitimate monarch, Richard II, and is crowned Henry IV. Following the murder of Richard (by a follower of Henry), Henry vows that he will make a pilgrimage to the Holy Land as penance. At the beginning of *1 Henry IV* Henry retains a sense of guilt and unease at having usurped the rightful monarch and having indirectly caused his death. The pilgrimage must be postponed because the country, and Henry's crown, is threatened by a group of rebels, formerly Henry's supporters. This challenge provides the opportunity for Prince Hal to undergo a radical transformation from wastrel to hero, finally winning his father's respect and killing Hotspur at the battle of Shrewsbury.

The first scene depicts a kingdom besieged from all sides as reports arrive of widespread rebellions. The king also has personal concerns – his son, heir to the throne, risks his reputation and is constantly embarrassing his father, who has more admiration for Hotspur, the gallant hero of the north. Meanwhile in the tavern, Hal's companion Falstaff plans a robbery with some others. Poins proposes to Hal that they double-cross their friends for a joke – robbing the robbers. Back at court Henry clashes with Hotspur who refuses to show respect for the king by giving up his prisoners; thus the seeds are sown for rebellion.

In the second act, various carriers are preparing for a journey while the thief Gadshill conspires with an employee of the inn. Falstaff and friends rob the travellers only to have Hal and Poins, in disguise, rob them. Meanwhile Hotspur resolves to rebel against the king and ignores his wife, who wants to know his secret business. Back at the tavern Falstaff weaves fabulous lies about how he fought the thieves, providing entertainment for both Hal and the audience. Hal and Falstaff then enact a play-within-a-play in which they alternate playing the role of the king, exploring the tensions underlying the relationships between father and son, and between Hal and Falstaff.

The tone of the third act darkens as events become more serious. The rebels meet in Wales and, using a map, purport to divide up the country between them. We are introduced to the legendary Glendower, and Lady Mortimer sings in Welsh before the rebels head off to fight the king. There is a crucial confrontation between father and son; Henry conveys his disappointment in Hal and lectures him on the need to distance himself from his future subjects. Hal promises to reform.

In Act 4, the rebels prepare for war at Shrewsbury and we hear of a transformed prince. Hotspur is undeterred and rouses his allies. Falstaff has been corrupt in his position as captain of a group of soldiers, accepting bribes from those wishing to avoid military service. The rebels debate military tactics and express their grievances to Sir Walter Blunt, the king's representative.

In the final act the king and rebels confront each other with mutual accusations. The king makes a final offer of mercy but Worcester keeps this information from the others. Falstaff contemplates, and is sceptical of, the honour to which Hotspur and Hal aspire. Hal's transformation is complete; he is a hero on the battlefield and, by killing Hotspur, obtains glory. Falstaff pretends to be dead to avoid being killed by Douglas and then attempts to claim the glory for having killed Hotspur. Hal has redeemed himself in his father's eyes and the rebellion is temporarily quelled. The play ends with the king's forces heading off to confront the remaining rebels, thus laying the groundwork for *2 Henry IV*.

Character summaries

Henry IV: fatigued from the burden of the crown; anxious at the threat of the rebels; suffering lingering guilt over Richard II; concerned about his wayward son.

Prince Hal: intelligent and shrewd; enjoys a carefree life among his drinking companions but is aware that this state is temporary; royal duty calls for his transformation and jealousy of Hotspur motivates his change to military hero and future monarch.

Lord John of Lancaster: younger son of Henry IV; brother to Hal.

Earl of Westmorland: kinsman to Henry IV.

Sir Walter Blunt: loyal follower of Henry IV.

Henry Percy, Earl of Northumberland: rebel against Henry IV; former ally.

Harry Hotspur: son of Henry Percy; rebel; high-spirited man of action with little patience for diplomacy; admired by Henry IV.

Lady (Kate) Percy: wife to Hotspur; sister to Lord Mortimer.

Thomas Percy, Earl of Worcester: Hotspur's uncle; rebel.

Edmund, Lord Mortimer: brother to Lady Percy; rebel; potential claimant to the throne.

Lady Mortimer: wife of Mortimer; daughter of Glendower.

Owen Glendower: Welsh; associated with magic and enchantment; father to Lady Mortimer; a rebel but doesn't fight at Shrewsbury.

Earl of Douglas: Scottish; rebel.

Sir Richard Vernon: Hotspur's cousin; rebel.

Richard Scroop, Archbishop of York: sympathetic to the rebels.

Sir John Falstaff: fat, indulgent, witty and boastful; thief and teller of tall tales; close friend of Hal.

Poins, Bardolph and Peto: Hal's companions at the tavern; petty criminals.

Mistress Quickly: hostess of the tavern in Eastcheap.

Francis: employee at the tavern.

BACKGROUND & CONTEXT

The play's setting – late medieval England

1 Henry IV, set in the early part of Henry IV's reign (1399–1413), relates to historical events in about 1402 and 1403. Shakespeare, writing in the late sixteenth century, is therefore imagining a much earlier time, the late medieval period. Henry IV was the first king from the House of Lancaster. The Lancastrians subsequently became embroiled in a long, drawn-out conflict (known as the Wars of the Roses) with the House of York, which also claimed the throne through the line of the deposed Richard II.

Shakespeare's historical context

The divine right of kings and the king's two bodies

Inherited from the medieval period was a strong belief that kings held their power according to divine right from God. The king was also thought to have 'two bodies', one mortal and human, and the other divine and immortal and which passed on to the successor. In *Richard II*, the king is not depicted as an ideal monarch. He seizes the estates of Henry Bolingbroke (who will become Henry IV), contrary to the customary laws of the kingdom, and is responsible for the murder of his own uncle, Thomas of Woodstock, Duke of Gloucester. Despite this, *Richard II* presents him as a type of martyr. During Richard's absence (the king having gone to Ireland to suppress a rebellion), Henry Bolingbroke returned from exile. Richard was subsequently deposed by him and then murdered.

Underlying the sympathetic attitude to Richard in *Richard II* is the assumption that an anointed king was God's representative on earth (although Shakespeare, throughout his work, questions this idea). This is also notable in some parts of *1 Henry IV*. The spectre of illegitimacy haunts Henry IV. He is not a monarch who came to the crown legitimately, thus Falstaff's exploits as a thief at the lower end of the social spectrum parallel the 'thieving' of the crown at the highest level.

Humours

The human body was thought to comprise four humours: blood, choler, melancholy and phlegm. Different characteristics were associated with each of these substances and it was thought that their proportions in a person dictated their personality. Imbalances in the humours were believed to cause adverse health effects and particular behaviours. In 1.3, when Hotspur angrily confronts the king, Northumberland cautions his son: 'What? Drunk with choler?' (1.3.127). Lady Percy observes Hotspur is 'altogether governed by humours' (3.1.228).

The position of women

In the early modern period women were perceived as socially and intellectually inferior to men. It was assumed women belonged in the home and they were generally excluded from warfare and matters of state. In trivialising his wife's concerns and questioning her trustworthiness, Hotspur reflects sixteenth-century views: 'Constant you are, / But yet a woman' (2.3.111–12). He claims he cannot trust her with an important secret because there are limits to how reliable women can be, simply because of their gender. Women were also associated with emotion (3.1.90–1).

Microcosm and macrocosm

An individual human was often imagined as a 'little world' (microcosm) reflecting the larger world of the cosmos (macrocosm). It was thought that there were analogies and correspondences between the two. This belief in correspondences, inherited from the medieval period, lies behind the tendency of Shakespeare to create links between events at the lower and upper levels of society. As you read the play, consider the ways in which scenes involving lower-class characters reflect events at the upper levels of society. Similarly, links are also created when Worcester admonishes Hotspur for his 'want of government' (3.1.178), suggesting that he is unable to control his temper, while also signalling his unfitness to govern others, despite his military prowess. As problematic as Henry's legitimacy is, the rebels do not necessarily represent a viable alternative.

The Seven Deadly Sins

In Shakespeare's period, human failings were often categorised as the 'Seven Deadly Sins'. These were: pride, gluttony, lust, wrath, sloth, avarice and envy. Humans were supposed to be moderate and temperate in their behaviours and appetites, an idea originating with Aristotle and adopted by Christian ideology. Falstaff embodies ungoverned appetite and is guilty of many of the Seven Deadly Sins. Also note how the rebels are guilty of pride, often considered the worst of the deadly sins: in 3.1 they arrogantly divide the map of England and Hotspur asserts that he will redirect a river to enhance his share. Hotspur is criticised by Worcester for his 'pride' (3.1.179) and is also frequently guilty of wrath; his colleagues urge him to be more moderate in his actions. Prince Hal has various models of behaviour around him and he must choose which to follow. Some scholars see the reformation of Hal as indebted to aspects of Christian ideology, mirroring the progress of man from a fallen state of sin to redemption through Christ. His ultimate rejection of Falstaff is thus like the repudiation of sin in order to follow a path of virtue.

The Vice and Morality Plays

Prior to Shakespeare's period, Morality, Mystery and Miracle Plays were common forms of drama. Mystery and Miracle Plays in the late Middle Ages depicted religious events and biblical stories. Morality Plays were didactic; that is, they were designed to teach people to act in virtuous ways using personifications of abstract ideas and human vices and virtues. A well-known Morality Play is *Everyman* (c. 1500). Although they became less popular from the mid sixteenth century, their influence can be noted in some later plays: for example, Christopher Marlowe's

Dr Faustus (c. 1588). In *1 Henry IV* Hal must choose between different types of behaviour, a theme indebted to the Morality Play tradition. In the Morality Plays, a popular figure was the Vice, whose function was to lead the central character astray; he was also a fool and often depicted on the Devil's back. Falstaff's character bears traces of this figure; he leads a wayward life and plays the fool. Although Falstaff claims that he will beat Hal away 'with a dagger of lath' (2.4.132), likening himself to Vice who carried such a weapon, Shakespeare's audience knew that at the end of a Morality Play it would be Vice who was beaten away. Falstaff thus foreshadows his own rejection by the prince in *2 Henry IV*.

Mythology

The English Renaissance period (from the late 1500s to 1660) was one of intense literary production that included a revival of interest in classical Greek and Roman literature. English Renaissance literature commonly refers to classical mythology, often focusing on tales of gods and goddesses. Such references may add grandeur to a figure; for example, in *1 Henry IV* the king compares Hotspur to Mars, the god of war (3.2.112), and Richard Vernon describes Hal as like Mercury (4.1.106) and his horse like Pegasus, the mythical flying horse (4.1.109). Sometimes such references are used for parody and comic effect; for example, Falstaff describes himself to be 'as valiant as Hercules' (2.4.264). Since Hercules was a hero who performed various amazing feats, Falstaff, of course, is nothing like him.

Magic

Owen Glendower is associated with magic (as is Wales generally). In Shakespeare's period there was widespread belief in magic (as well as scepticism, as expressed by Hotspur in 3.1). Some people purported to be able to communicate with and command spirits, as Glendower does (3.1.50, 53), and customers would pay for love potions, spells to cause harm and other magical services. Such beliefs often led to the persecution of people as witches and many so accused in Europe were executed.

The publication history of *1 Henry IV*

There are no surviving draft manuscripts, notes or diaries left by Shakespeare so scholars have to piece together other evidence to determine a publication date for *1 Henry IV*. The play is believed to have been written around 1596 and first performed in 1596 or 1597. It is a sequel to the earlier play *Richard II* (1595). Scholars debate whether Shakespeare was planning the future narratives of *2 Henry IV* and *Henry V* when he wrote *1 Henry IV*. The play can be studied on its own, or in the context of the tetralogy as a whole. It continues some ideas and themes from *Richard II* and has ideas that will continue on in *2 Henry IV*, the next play in the series.

There were various quarto editions (small books made by folding sheets of paper four times) published between 1596 and 1623, when the First Folio (a collection of most of Shakespeare's plays) was published. The Folio edition of the play drew its text mainly from the 1613 quarto although its compilers censored all oaths (swearing on the name of God or Christ), following the Act to Restrain the Abuses of Players (1606).

GENRE, STRUCTURE & LANGUAGE

Genre

In the 1623 First Folio, the editors divided the plays into three genres: comedies, tragedies and histories. *1 Henry IV* is a history; that is, it draws from some factual events and actual figures from history and weaves a story around them. At the same time, it is dramatic fiction. Shakespeare often alters historical facts, the ages and names of people or the sequence of events in order to achieve particular dramatic effects. For example, Hotspur's real wife was named Elizabeth, not Kate, and although the historical Hotspur was much older than Hal, Shakespeare makes them of similar age (3.2.103) in order to emphasise their rivalry. Shakespeare also creates completely fictional dialogues between characters and develops particular personas for characters that most likely are very different from the personalities of the actual historical figures.

Shakespeare drew from several sources in obtaining his basic storyline and ideas for characters; these included Raphael Holinshed's *Chronicles of England, Scotland, and Ireland* (1577), Samuel Daniel's *The First Four Books of the Civil Wars* (1595) and an anonymous play *The Famous Victories of Henry V* (1594).

In the past, history was generally seen as a series of facts, based on the assumption that historians could arrive at 'the truth' about what had occurred. More recently, some theorists and critics have suggested that there is always an element of narrative to history and that the 'truth' is always relative, depending on from whose point of view a story is being told. According to this view, there is always an element of fiction to our understanding of the past; Shakespeare's historical imagination can be considered in this light. He was not purporting to present historical truth; rather, his history plays invited the audience to speculate on the issues and events that affected historical figures, whether they were monarchs or ordinary people. What conversations might have taken place? What emotions might these people have experienced? Shakespeare's history plays were radical because they gave ordinary people the illusion that they were witnessing the inner workings of government, and the thoughts and actions of those with the power to affect the lives of others.

Structure

The play is constructed of multiple scenes set in various locations, with frequent shifts between the interwoven plots generating dramatic energy. Scenes set in London, Wales, Kent, Northumberland and Shrewsbury create geographical variety while class differences are conveyed by scenes set at court and the tavern in Eastcheap. This creates a sense of the depth and breadth of English society.

The different scenes at first seem disparate, but are connected in several ways. For example, the scene of the robbery at Gad's Hill resonates politically with the suggestion that Henry IV 'stole' the crown, thus linking him with the ordinary thieves. The effect of 2.3 is to remind the audience of the developing conspiracy – the rebels are about to attempt to 'rob the robber' by deposing Henry. Shakespeare thus creates parallels between events at the upper and lower levels of society.

In 2.4 there is a 'play-within-a-play', where Hal and Falstaff's role-playing articulates the simmering tensions underlying the various relationships. The play-within-a-play is a common dramatic device that Shakespeare uses in many of his works, for example: *Hamlet, A Midsummer Night's Dream* and *The Taming of the Shrew*. The effect of this device is often described as 'metadramatic' or 'metatheatrical' because it draws attention to the process of drama and the nature of theatre itself. It reminds the audience that they are watching a play, thus temporarily breaking the illusion of the world that the play creates.

The first two acts depict the growing rebellion contrasted with the comic, free life in the tavern. Then, from Act 3, there is a shift to a more serious tone as the rebellion gets underway, and there are scenes that take place on the battlefield. Play turns to war as Prince Hal undergoes the metamorphosis from wastrel to hero. With the shift, some characters seem out of place; for example, Falstaff is at home in the tavern but not on the battlefield. What is funny elsewhere, such as Falstaff's thieving, takes on a more sinister element here when he corruptly takes bribes from those wanting to avoid war.

In the latter part of the play, particularly from Act 4 onwards, the scenes become shorter, making the shifts between the different groups of characters and sides of the conflict more rapid. This accelerates the pace of the play, creating momentum and greater dramatic tension as it builds towards the dramatic climax of Hal's fight with Hotspur.

Language

Shakespeare was a gifted wordsmith, inventing many new words (such as 'skimble-skamble', 3.1.148) and playing on the multiple meanings of a word. Shifts in a conversation often hinge on a word used in one sense by one character, then in a different sense by another. His language can be difficult when encountered for the first time; some words, which were common at the time, are now unfamiliar. This is particularly evident in scenes such as 2.1 where there are many terms that were predominantly used by the ordinary workers. Other words may be familiar but their meanings have changed over time, which can be misleading; the vocabulary lists will help you to interpret the intended meaning.

Shakespeare's syntax (the order of words) can also be challenging. It is more important to try and gain an overall sense of a passage than to understand each component. Watching a play or a film will help you, since body language, gesture and tone of voice all add meaning. Also, reading the play more than once will help; with each reading you will gain new insights and greater understanding of how Shakespeare's language works.

You will notice Shakespeare's frequent use of metaphors to describe people, emotions and events. This technique, common in Renaissance literature, adds depth and complexity to the language of the play through the mental images that the words evoke. For example, notice how, in order to create discord and animosity towards Henry IV, Hotspur reframes Richard II through metaphors. Richard is 'that sweet lovely rose' (1.3.173), whereas Henry is a 'thorn' and 'canker' (1.3.174). The metaphors suggest that Richard as the 'rose' is the rightful plant of the garden (the state), while Henry is the illegitimate ruler, the weed or worm that has infected this rose, the true ruler of England.

In *1 Henry IV*, language is important in conveying a sense of the diverse places, people and cultures of Britain. These differences can be a source of conflict; for example, Hotspur is scornful of the Welsh language – to speak Welsh, according to insular English views, was to speak nonsense (3.1.47). There are variations in language not only between places but also between the social classes: note the differences in language between the scenes at court and in the tavern. Language is also important in conveying the respect or disrespect that various characters have for each other. Note how Hotspur conveys his antagonism towards the king by describing him as 'this vile politician Bolingbroke' (1.3.238), which challenges the respect he owes a sovereign and thus anticipates the rebellion against Henry IV (also see Glendower at 3.1.60).

Comedy is an important aspect of the language in *1 Henry IV*, particularly in the speeches of Falstaff in his dialogues with Hal and their tavern companions. Much of the humour arises from the various insults that the characters direct at each other: 'Peace, ye fat-guts', says Hal to Falstaff (2.2.30) and 'how long is't ago, Jack, since thou sawest thine own knee?' (2.4.320–1). Some of the insults are ironic; that is, they mean the opposite of their apparent meaning, such as when Hal calls Falstaff 'lean Jack' and 'bare-bone' (2.4.319). Also note how comic elements are created through Falstaff's speech. Sometimes they arise from the way he initially sets up an expectation from a word, and then swiftly changes its meaning. For example, his phrase 'men of good government' (1.2.27) conveys respectability; however, this changes as he continues 'being governed as the sea is, by our noble and chaste mistress the moon, under whose countenance we steal' (1.2.27–9). Humour arises from the swift change of meaning. At the same time, the reference to government and thievery in close proximity resonates with the implicit cloud over Henry IV's legitimacy as a monarch.

Sometimes the wordplay draws on similar sounding words or phrases, e.g. 'were it not here apparent that thou art heir apparent' (1.2.56–7). Falstaff plays on similar sounding phrases or uses a word in different ways: 'here lies the point – why, being son to me, art thou so pointed at?' (2.4.399–400). Similarly, Worcester says that 'To save our heads' they will need to raise 'a head' [an army] (1.3.278).

As you are reading the play, note the rhythm of the language. Most of the upper-class characters speak in verse, while the lower-class characters speak in prose. The verse lines are in iambic pentameter – there are five 'beats' or stresses to the line with unstressed syllables in between. This pattern gives a sense of overall order. Changes between prose and verse can be used to create particular effects; Hal in the tavern in the early parts of the play speaks in prose, suggesting his affinity with the lower-class characters, whereas in the latter part of the play, after his transformation, he speaks in verse. In some conversations between characters you will note that their speeches seem connected. The two speeches together create a single line of iambic pentameter, forming five beats between them. This unity of rhythm parallels particular connections between characters at certain points. For example, when the tavern gang are about to commit their robbery, Gadshill says 'There's enough to make us all –' (2.2.56); Falstaff finishes the line with 'To be hanged' (2.2.57). Together the speeches create one line of iambic pentameter and by finishing the line Falstaff changes the meaning from triumph to doom.

You may also notice that some lines seem to 'stand out' from the text as memorable quotations which could be used outside of the play, such as Falstaff's 'the better part of valour is discretion' (5.4.118–19). In Shakespeare's time, proverbs and aphorisms were popular; these were short sayings, usually with a didactic function (trying to teach a moral lesson). Shakespeare's audience often took notes of useful lines they could add to their commonplace books (compilations of useful sayings).

SCENE-BY-SCENE ANALYSIS

Act 1

1.1 Summary: *Henry IV postpones his pilgrimage to the Holy Land as reports arrive of rebellion in the kingdom. He is concerned about his wayward son Hal but admires Hotspur.*

Henry IV, beleaguered and careworn, announces that internal conflict will cease and that he will embark on a pilgrimage. These plans are dashed by reports of conflict throughout the kingdom: Glendower to the west has defeated 'the noble Mortimer' (1.1.38–40), and 'the gallant Hotspur' threatens the north (1.1.52). The king reflects on the shortcomings of Hal and expresses admiration for Hotspur, whom he enviously wishes were his own son.

1.2 Summary: *Hal banters with Falstaff. Poins plans the robbery of some rich pilgrims and traders, then proposes that he and Hal play a trick on Falstaff by robbing the robbers.*

The action moves from the gravity of matters of state to a comic scene, usually set in the tavern, in which Prince Hal engages in verbal banter with Sir John Falstaff. Falstaff's language is not deferential; he addresses the prince as 'Hal' not 'Prince Hal' and calls him 'lad', suggesting Hal is Falstaff's inferior. Hal knows Falstaff well, yet is tolerant of his foibles at this early stage. Hal mocks Falstaff's lifestyle, which comprises frivolous activities: drinking, theft and womanising. Asking Falstaff, 'Where shall we take a purse tomorrow' (1.2.98), Hal appears to include himself as a thief yet when Poins asks Hal directly if he will be a thief, Hal says no. Poins proposes they rob some pilgrims heading to Canterbury and some traders bound for London. The reference to traders reminds us that London was rapidly developing as a place of trade and commerce in the early modern period.

The thieves are confident that Hal is on their side and will not betray them and Falstaff pressures him to take part in the robbery. After Falstaff leaves, Poins suggests a joke they can play on the others: after Falstaff and his band have committed the robbery, he and Hal will rob the robbers. The jest will be in the 'incomprehensible lies' (1.2.184) Falstaff will tell by way of explanation.

In a soliloquy, Hal reveals his inner thoughts and confesses that he will only tolerate his companions' behaviour 'awhile' and that his eventual reformation will appear all the more wondrous because of his earlier faults (1.2.193–215).

1.3 Summary: *Henry demands Hotspur's prisoners but Hotspur refuses; rebellion stirs. Hotspur's hot-headed nature is evident as he fails to listen to Worcester.*

At court, the king confronts the rebels. His words, 'I will from henceforth rather be myself' (1.3.5), echo Hal's similar resolution at the end of the previous scene. The king fears he has been too lenient, and has encouraged rebellion; he intends again to become 'Mighty, and to be feared' (1.3.6). Worcester complains that the king is not treating the rebels well – the Percys helped to make Henry great, and expected to be rewarded accordingly. The king is furious at this lack of respect: 'I do see / Danger and disobedience in thine eye' (1.3.14–15).

He is also furious with Hotspur, who has refused the demand from the king's representative to surrender the prisoners taken at Holmedon during the recent battle. Hotspur explains that it was not the demand itself that he refused but rather the king's effeminate messenger, whose appearance and behaviour was disdainful of the brutal realities of the battlefield. Hotspur is short-tempered and has no time for impractical, courtly types.

Hotspur's refusal to give up the prisoners is a challenge to the king's authority. He proposes to take as a prisoner for ransom Hotspur's brother-in-law Mortimer, whom, he claims, has 'revolted' (1.3.91). Hotspur is, as his name suggests, liable to do and say things in the heat of the moment and after the king exits, Hotspur's father, Northumberland, urges him not to act hastily. Hotspur expresses his disrespect for the king by shifting his language from 'unthankful King' (1.3.134), to 'ingrate and cankered Bolingbroke' (1.3.135). Using the name by which Henry was known before he was king conveys Hotspur's rebellious intentions.

Hotspur suggests that Henry IV was 'trembling even at the name of Mortimer' (1.3.142), because Mortimer was proclaimed by Richard II as heir to the throne. Northumberland expresses guilt for their part in Richard's usurpation and Worcester adds: 'for whose death we in the world's wide mouth / Live scandalized and foully spoken of' (1.3.151–2). Hotspur rouses the others to anger: 'for his sake [we] wear the detested blot / Of murderous subornation' (1.3.160–1) arguing that their reputations have suffered from having assisted Henry to gain the crown. Worcester attempts to calm him, unimpressed by Hotspur's inability to listen to anyone. Northumberland also chastises his son for 'Tying thine ear to no tongue but thine own!' (1.3.235). Worcester instructs Hotspur to deliver the prisoners and directs Northumberland to go to the Archbishop of York; the words 'secretly' and 'creep' (1.3.262) convey the clandestine nature of the developing revolt against the king. Worcester suggests that the Archbishop nurses a grievance against the king.

Key point

In 1.2, the proposed theft from pilgrims is particularly unsettling since these are people on a religious mission. This invites comparison with Henry IV's theft of the crown from Richard II, God's appointee. It also reminds the audience of Henry IV's intention to go on a pilgrimage to ease his conscience. Similarly the reference to the theft of 'crowns' (1.2.130) reminds the audience of the larger theft of the crown that haunts the play. The proposed robbery of the robbers also resonates at the political level; Henry IV, having stolen the crown from Richard II, is currently at risk of having the crown stolen from him by the rebels.

Key vocabulary

Coz (1.1.90): cousin

Sack (1.2.7): wine

Leaping-houses (1.2.9): brothels

Phoebus (1.2.15): the sun

Grace (1.2.17): refinement; the favour of God; majesty; the prayer before a meal. When Falstaff says Hal will not have sufficient grace as would precede a simple meal, it suggests that Hal, like his father, does not have the natural favour of God because they are not natural successors to the throne.

Marry (1.2.23): a mild oath – 'Mary' (not blasphemous)

Squires of the night's body (1.2.24): attendants on the night. (This personifies the night and puns on attendants of a knight.)

Diana (1.2.25): classical goddess of the moon, hunting and chastity. (While the latter is not relevant to Falstaff, as a thief he goes hunting by moonlight.)

Gentlemen of the shade (1.2.26): thieves; this is ironic in its use of 'gentlemen' as it gives thieves a nobility they don't have.

The moon's men (1.2.31): thieves; some scholars also see this as a reference to the favourite courtiers of Elizabeth I, whose fortunes were changeable depending on the queen's whim. Elizabeth was commonly described as the goddess Diana, because of her chastity. Monarchs often took on, or were given by those wishing to flatter them, associations with classical gods and heroic historical figures.

Lay by (1.2.35): a robber's command

Old lad of the castle (1.2.41–2): a pun on the original name of Falstaff's character, Sir John Oldcastle. Shakespeare was forced to change the name after objections from relatives of Oldcastle, the historical figure who may have inspired the character.

Buff jerkin (1.2.42): close-fitting leather jacket worn by soldiers

Wag (1.2.44): habitual joker

Pox (1.2.47): venereal disease

Old Father Antic the law (1.2.60): an Antic was a clown in Tudor drama. Falstaff speaks of the law as a clown, which echoes the suggestion of Falstaff as a judge (1.2.64).

'Sblood (1.2.73): God's blood (an oath)

Vanity (1.2.82): worldly things. Its use here by Falstaff is humorous and ironic since Falstaff is only ever concerned with worldly things.

Wisdom cries out in the streets and no man regards it (1.2.88–9): an allusion to a biblical passage in Proverbs 1:20, 24.

Damnable iteration (1.2.90): the Devil's ability to quote from the Bible (that is, the ability to quote from the Bible doesn't make you a saint).

Set a match (1.2.106–7): plan a robbery

Cozening (1.2.121): cheating

Gad's Hill (1.2.124): place notorious for robberies

Vizards (1.2.126): masks

Eastcheap (1.2.129): a tavern in the area of Eastcheap, the setting for 2.4, and often 1.2; also known as the Boar's Head

Crowns (1.2.130): coins

Yedward (1.2.132): Edward (Poins)

Misprision (1.3.26): misunderstanding

Earl of March (1.3.83): Mortimer

Choler (1.3.127): one of the four humours; associated with anger

Zounds (1.3.129): God's wounds (an oath)

The unhappy King (1.3.146): Richard II

Soft (1.3.153): wait

Figures (1.3.207): figures of speech

King of smiles (1.3.243): a king of false appearance

Ravenspurgh (1.3.244–5): harbour in Yorkshire, where Henry Bolingbroke landed upon returning from exile

Cozeners (1.3.251): deceivers

Thou still lettest slip (1.3.272): Northumberland is criticising his son for not staying in control, for being too impetuous.

Head (1.3.278): army

Q How does the robbery proposed by Hal's companions parallel the political situation?

Q Analyse the characters Hal and Falstaff based on their dialogues in 1.2.

Act 2

2.1 Summary: *Carriers prepare for the day's journey. A conspiracy is established between Gadshill and the Chamberlain who, in exchange for a fee, provides information to thieves on potential travellers to rob.*

The scene conveys the hard life and poverty of the ordinary people and contrasts it with the carefree attitude in the temporary haven of the tavern. Widespread poverty, often exacerbated by bad harvests and food shortages, caused suffering, disease and early death, and created motivation for crime. The language in this scene is full of slang, much of which is unfamiliar to us now. We are also given information about working conditions. It is 4 am and already people are up for work. We hear about price rises and food shortages; the previous ostler (the man responsible for preparing the horses for travellers) died, which the First Carrier attributes to the price of oats rising. The workers also have to deal with fleas; they complain of being bitten all over.

We gain a sense of the risks to travellers and traders. Gadshill, a notorious thief, obtains information regarding the property and destination of guests at the inn from the Chamberlain (a servant) as he, along with Hal, Falstaff and his companions, intend to waylay and rob them. The Chamberlain will be given a share of the spoils. The Chamberlain calls Gadshill 'pick-purse' (2.1.49) but Gadshill retorts that the Chamberlain is just as bad since he aids and abets the robberies: 'thou variest no more from picking of purses than giving direction doth from labouring. Thou layest the plot how' (2.1.51–3).

2.2 Summary: *The robbers are robbed. Hal and Poins double-cross Falstaff and the others, setting the scene for some tall tales by Falstaff.*

Hal and Poins hide from Falstaff, who comically exaggerates his distress at the deprivation of his horse and having to walk. Falstaff utters the memorable line 'I am accursed to rob in that thief's company' (2.2.10). His humorous complaint is that Poins is an inferior thief and that Falstaff thus suffers by having to work with him.

Hal tells Falstaff to lie down on the ground and listen for the oncoming travellers they will rob. Falstaff jokes about his size, asking if Hal has levers to lift him up again, and also about the prospect of stealing from the king. When the others enter and Gadshill says 'Stand!' (2.2.47), (the common demand of a highwayman) Falstaff puns on this, replying 'So I do, against my will' (2.2.48) – that is, he is standing involuntarily because they took his horse away. It is comic, and surreal, that Hal, the king's son, is treated as one of the thieves about to steal from his own father. The travellers arrive and Falstaff and the others rob them; Hal and Poins re-enter, disguised, and 'rob the thieves' (2.2.92), who run away, leaving the money.

2.3 Summary: *Hotspur contemplates a letter urging caution. Lady Percy tries in vain to gain his confidence.*

Hotspur contemplates a letter; the writer is unspecified but its function is to provide an opportunity for Hotspur to express his thoughts. It urges caution but Hotspur is dismissive. Lady Percy complains of her husband's neglect and preoccupation. She says that in his sleep Hotspur cries out with the language of war and observes that his 'spirit ... hath been so at war' (2.3.58). This reflects the imminent state of England, at war with itself. Hotspur doesn't take his wife's concerns seriously, teasing her; when she asks him 'What is it carries you away?' (2.3.78) he pretends to take her literally: 'Why, my horse, my love, my horse' (2.3.79). He rejects the quiet domestic life in favour of the battlefield and refuses to tell Kate his secrets. For a moment, he appears to trust her – 'for I well believe / Thou wilt not utter –' (2.3.113–14) but finishes the sentence with 'what thou dost not know' (2.3.114). If he doesn't tell her his plan, she can't possibly disclose it.

2.4 Summary: *Hal cruelly teases Francis, an employee of the tavern. Hal and Poins enjoy their joke on Falstaff as he fabricates the tale of the theft from the thieves. Through a play-within-a-play Hal and Falstaff articulate the underlying tensions of their relationship and of Hal's relationship with his father.*

Hal is at home at the tavern among the ordinary drinkers. He learns the colloquial language and revels in his ability with language: 'I am so good a proficient in one quarter of an hour that I can drink with any tinker in his own language during my life' (2.4.17–19). Note that Hal's speech is in prose, not the verse that is usual for the upper classes in Shakespeare's plays. Hal teases Francis by creating a conflict between the inexperienced waiter's duty to the prince and his duty to the customers. This humour shows a cruel streak in Hal.

Hal delights in language. He insults the vintner in a barrage of words: 'Wilt thou rob this leathern-jerking, crystal-button, not-pated, agate-ring, puke-stocking, caddis-garter, smooth-tongue Spanish pouch?' (2.4.67–9), confusing Francis with an excess of slang terms. Hal also parodies Hotspur for his delight in bloody battles: 'he that kills me some six or seven dozen of Scots at a breakfast, washes his hands, and says to his wife, "Fie upon this quiet life, I want work"' (2.4.101–3). Hal's hyperbole is comic, as is his ironic description of excessive killing as a 'quiet life'.

Falstaff arrives, angry that their theft was thwarted when they were robbed themselves. He complains that 'There is nothing but roguery to be found in villainous man' (2.4.120–1). Humour arises from Falstaff's hypocrisy in complaining of being robbed. Falstaff accuses Hal and Poins of cowardice, for running away when thieves attacked the robber band (unaware, of course, that Hal and Poins were the thieves).

Falstaff's constant lies and exaggerations are comic as Hal and the others know he is a liar and a rogue. He claims he has not had a drink that day (2.4.147) to which Hal laughingly retorts: 'Thy lips are scarce wiped since thou drunkest last' (2.4.148–9). Falstaff then proceeds to report on the robbery of the robbers. Hal and Poins delight in his fabrications and enjoy the spectacle of Falstaff's performance. He claims that he fought 'with a dozen of them two hours together' (2.4.159–60) and suffered multiple blows and injuries, which Hal knows to be completely fictitious. There is immense comic attraction in Falstaff's untruthful claim to value 'truth' (2.4.166). Not only does he fabricate the story, his story continually changes. He supports his assertions of the truth of things that are patently false by declaring that if they are not true, then he is something he's not (a 'Jew', 2.4.174; 'a bunch of radish', 2.4.181). Amusingly, some of the comparisons are true, for example 'or I am a villain else' (2.4.202). In Falstaff's tale the number of alleged thieves that attacked him grows and Hal observes that the tale becomes 'monstrous' (2.4.15). Hal and Falstaff pour colourful insults on each other in a battle of words ('huge hill of flesh', 2.4.239; 'you elf-skin, you dried neat's-tongue', 2.4.240–1). This verbal duelling invites comparison with Hal's subsequent physical battle with Hotspur.

Hal then confronts Falstaff with the truth. Falstaff quickly shifts his story, claiming that he knew it was the prince all along and was unable to kill the heir to the throne. Pleased that Hal has the money, he proposes to celebrate with a play wherein he will play the king and Hal will practise how he will answer his father (2.4.368). When Hal suggests they swap roles, Falstaff says 'Depose me?' (2.4.424). The innocent swapping of actors' roles is given an ominous tone – Henry IV obtained the crown by deposing Richard, and it is now under imminent threat. The play-within-a-play is an important device that enables Hal and Falstaff to explore both the relationship between royal father and son and also the problems with their friendship. The role-playing articulates tensions that will erupt in later stages of the play and in *2 Henry IV*. Falstaff, acting as the king, accurately conveys both the king's concerns about his son and Falstaff's own anxieties about what will happen to their relationship when Hal is king. Falstaff is painfully aware that Hal's association with the tavern group is irreconcilable with his future role as monarch and Hal's role-playing of the king shows his recognition that, in becoming king, he will need to break away from his friends. Nevertheless, when the sheriff arrives, Hal protects them, telling his friends to hide. The act ends on the ominous note that they 'must all to the wars' (2.4.528–9). Events will take a more serious turn in Act 3. There is an element of cruelty in Hal's resolution to put Falstaff in charge of infantry (2.4.530), which suggests that Hal is exacting a penalty for Falstaff's behaviour. Hal resolves that 'The money shall be paid back again with advantage' (2.4.531–2) which again signals that the time for joking is over; serious events and questions now need to be faced.

Key point

In 2.2, the Chamberlain gives Gadshill information facilitating the robbery and in return Gadshill assures him that 'thou shalt have a share in our purchase, as I am a true man' (2.1.92–3). The irony is that Gadshill is not a 'true man' so there is, of course, no guarantee that he will keep his word. The Chamberlain recognises this: 'Nay, rather let me have it as you are a false thief' (2.1.94–5). The episode resonates at the political level by echoing the sentiments of the rebels in the previous scene. If Henry IV 'stole' the crown, aided by the rebels, they, like the Chamberlain, expected to receive a reward in return. Their complaint is that the king has not kept his part of the bargain. The idea is emphasised further in the next scene when Falstaff says 'A plague upon it when thieves cannot be true one to another!' (2.2.26–7). Here it is highly comical because Falstaff is insisting on honesty within thievery, loyalty within betrayal.

Key vocabulary

Few flocks in the point (2.1.6): wool stuffing in the saddle to make it softer

Jade (2.1.6): worn-out horse

House (2.1.10): inn

First cock (2.1.19): midnight

Jordan (2.1.21): chamber pot

Chamber-lye (2.1.22): urine

Ostler (2.1.23): the role of the ostler was to prepare the horses for travellers and help them on their way.

Great charge (2.1.47): substantial money or goods

Franklin (2.1.55): rich landowner

Marks (2.1.56): a weight in gold

Saint Nicholas' clerks (2.1.62–3): slang for highwayman; Saint Nicholas was the patron saint of travellers.

Profession (2.1.72): refers to the 'profession' of highwaymen; ironic in giving the practice the appearance of respectability

Foot-landrakers (2.1.74): vagabond thieves on foot

Long-staff sixpenny strikers (2.1.74–5): thieves on foot who would hold up a man for sixpence.

Strike (2.1.78): rob

Fern-seed (2.1.88): thought to be invisible except on St John's Eve (Midsummer's Night). If gathered on that night it was thought to confer invisibility on whoever carried it.

Break my wind (2.2.13): be breathless; fart

Forsworn (2.2.15): rejected; denied

Peach (2.2.43): inform against you (to save oneself)

Ballads (2.2.44): songs composed to mark special occasions printed on broadsides (single sheets of paper) and sold in the streets. Music was not printed with them but they might indicate a popular tune to go with the words.

Case ye (2.2.51): disguise yourself

Basilisks (2.3.55): large cannons named after a mythical beast, the basilisk, whose breath or look was fatal

Culverin (2.3.55): smallest size cannon

Esperance (2.3.74): Percy's motto means hope

Spleen (2.3.81): the spleen was associated with sudden action and emotion, thus irritability

His title (2.3.85): Mortimer's supposed claim to the throne

Cracked crowns (2.3.96): suggests the imminent attack on Henry IV, but also refers to currency – crowns were five-shilling pieces

Pass them current (2.3.97): pass them (counterfeit coins) as if they were legal tender. This alludes to the idea of Henry as a counterfeit king.

Hogsheads (2.4.5): the casks; special customers were invited to drink in the cellar amid the casks.

Drawers (2.4.7): staff at the tavern employed to serve the drinks

Dyeing scarlet (2.4.15): drinking, resulting in a red complexion

Anon, anon, sir (2.4.25): coming sir

Pint of bastard (2.4.26): sweet Spanish wine

Michaelmas (2.4.53): 29 September, feast of St Michael the archangel

Parcel of a reckoning (2.4.100): items making up a bill. Hal means that Francis has no eloquence; his speech is as mundane as a bill.

Titan (2.4.116): the sun (Falstaff's red cheeks)

Lime (2.4.120): Falstaff is complaining that lime has been added to his wine.

I would I were a weaver: I could sing psalms (2.4.128–9): Falstaff muses that he will become a weaver and sing psalms. Weavers often sang at their work and, since many of them were Puritans, they sang religious songs. After the Protestant Reformation of the Christian Church, in which Protestants distinguished themselves from Catholics, there were further splits within Protestantism. Puritans advocated more simple religious rituals and church services, rejected religious art as idolatry and took a dim view of the theatres, seeing them as ungodly and liable to lead people to sin.

Dagger of lath (2.4.132): a wooden sword. Falstaff imagines himself as Vice, the character associated with temptation and the Devil in the old Morality Plays.

Ere (2.4.141): before

Ecce signum (2.4.163–4): Latin for 'behold the evidence'

Kendal green (2.4.218): a cloth of green worn by foresters and often associated with thieves; Robin Hood's men were said to wear Kendal green.

Strappado; racks (2.4.233): instruments of torture

Sanguine (2.4.238): red; drink-flushed in the face

Elf-skin (2.4.240): nothing

Bull's-pizzle (2.4.241): bull's penis

Out-faced (2.4.251): separated; out-manoeuvred

Hercules (2.4.264): classical hero

Argument (2.4.274): plot

State (2.4.371): chair of state; the throne

Tickle-brain (2.4.390–1): strong drink

Micher (2.4.401): truant; someone who doesn't do their duties

A charge of foot (2.4.530): an infantry company

Q What information is the audience given in 2.1 about the working conditions of ordinary people in Shakespeare's time (which he draws on to imagine the early fifteenth century)?

Q Analyse the play-within-a-play scene in 2.4 where Falstaff and Hal play different roles. What does it reveal about their relationship?

Act 3

3.1 Summary: *The rebels meet in Wales and, anticipating victory, proceed to divide up the country using a map, like thieves divvying up the spoils. Lady Mortimer sings in Welsh; the agreement is signed and they head off.*

The rebels meet to determine how they will divide the kingdom after defeating Henry IV. Here we get a sense of the magical associations of Wales and the character of Owen Glendower. Hotspur responds to Glendower's magical representation of himself with a cynical pragmatism, resulting in some comic lines. When Glendower claims that he 'can call spirits from the vasty deep' (3.1.50), Hotspur, refusing to take the claim seriously, retorts: 'Why, so can I, or so can any man: / But will they come when you do call for them?' (3.1.51– 2). Hotspur refuses to take Glendower's claims seriously. Disagreements within the group over the three-way division of the kingdom reflect the potential for internal conflict.

Glendower produces the map and proposes that they divide it three ways: Mortimer will receive the southern portion of England, Glendower the western section of Wales beyond the Severn river, and Hotspur the northern section from the river Trent. Hotspur complains that his share is not equal to that of the others, using the word 'rob' (3.1.101), another reminder that the rebels are proposing to rob the monarch of his crown. Hotspur's impetuous nature is foregrounded; he has no patience with Glendower's tales of magic and mystery. Mortimer and Worcester chasten Hotspur, urging him to be moderate and control his temper. Worcester complains of his 'want of government' (3.1.178).

The scene conveys ideas about the Welsh people and their language. The love between Mortimer and his wife has to overcome the language barrier (3.1.187). Hotspur is scornful of the Welsh language: 'Let me not understand you then, speak it in Welsh' (3.1.115), yet the group of rebels and we, the audience, are captivated when Mortimer's wife, Glendower's daughter, sings a song in Welsh, accompanied by magical musicians that

Glendower has conjured from the air (3.1.218–20). Music brings out the softer side in all of them and the scene ends with loving banter between Hotspur and his wife Kate. The rebels sign their agreement and head off, with the exception of Glendower who is 'not ready yet' (3.1.83).

3.2 Summary: *Hal faces his father. The king conveys his disappointment in his son and gives him advice on how a monarch should act. Hal promises to reform and to prove himself worthy by taking on Hotspur.*

In this tense confrontation between father and son, king and prince, Henry refers to Hal as the Prince of Wales (3.2.1), the traditional title of the heir to the throne; this reminds Hal of his duty. Henry lists Hal's offences and the consequences of his behaviour – the prince has lost his place at the Council and is alienated from the court. He chastises his son for mixing with the ordinary people and thus, rather than appearing mysterious and remote as befits an heir to the throne, is seen as ordinary. Henry compares this with his own behaviour – by being rarely seen he is wondered at 'like a comet' (3.2.47). His crown and the esteem of the people were 'won by rareness' (3.2.59).

Note Henry's phrase: 'And then I stole all courtesy from heaven' (3.2.50). He refers to his taking on the divine authority of a monarch, yet the word 'stole' reminds the audience that he did not legitimately inherit the crown. 'Dressed myself' (3.2.51) suggests role-playing, rather than true humility, and 'pluck allegiance' (3.2.52) suggests taking something rather than earning it. Henry depicts Richard II as frivolous – a 'skipping King' (3.2.60) – and derides the former monarch for associating 'with shallow jesters' (3.2.61) and for mingling 'his royalty with capering fools' (3.2.63). In this way Henry warns Hal about mixing with fools such as Falstaff; to do so puts the crown at risk. He also compares Hal with Richard in being seen too often; Richard was 'daily swallowed by men's eyes' (3.2.70) so no longer regarded as extraordinary. Henry laments Hal's 'vile participation' (3.2.87) in the ordinary world.

Hal can hardly get a word in; he can only humbly promise that he will thereafter 'Be more myself' (3.2.93). He blames his wayward behaviour on his youth and asserts he is capable of reform. Just as Henry compares Hal with Richard II, he also compares himself to Hotspur. He suggests that Hotspur is more worthy to be the heir than Hal (3.2.98–9), presenting the radical suggestion that it is merit, not title, that should earn the crown.

In using the word 'shadow' Henry's comment reminds the audience of Hal's earlier promise that he would, like a sun obscured by the clouds, emerge in greater splendour (1.2.193–215). Henry conveys the threat posed by the rebels (3.2.118–19) yet he asserts that Hal's behaviour renders him his 'nearest and dearest enemy' (3.2.123). This rouses Hal and he promises to redeem his reputation by defeating Hotspur and thus prove himself worthy of being Henry's son and a future monarch. Hal speaks of gaining honour as an exchange of Hotspur's 'glorious deeds' for Hal's 'indignities' (3.2.145–6). Henry is impressed with Hal and places his trust in him. Blunt enters to report that the rebels will meet at Shrewsbury; Henry commands that they are all to set out to confront the rebels.

3.3 Summary: *Falstaff is dejected and reflects on his life. He complains of having his pocket picked but Hal takes the side of the Hostess.*

Back in the tavern Falstaff is in low spirits, feeling that he has declined in health since recent events. He resolves to repent (thus mirroring Hal's resolution in the previous scene), ironically complaining of 'villainous company' (3.3.9), and Bardolph's reply is just as comical, observing that Falstaff in this state will not live long. Falstaff calls for a bawdy song to cheer him up (thus forgetting his resolution to repent his ways). He reflects on his life and behaviour. His speech is humorous because he frames his behaviour as moderate but then subverts the expectation with various confessions.

The light-hearted banter and comical quarrelling give way to a more serious tone when Falstaff refers to the two aspects of Hal; while he does not fear him as a man, 'as thou art prince, I fear thee' (3.3.144). Hal's insults also have a more cutting edge now: 'Art thou not ashamed?' (3.3.160–1). Falstaff excuses himself as having 'more flesh' (3.3.165) and therefore being more likely to sin (since it was thought virtue resided in the soul and vice in the flesh). Hal reports that he has paid back the stolen money and tells Falstaff that he has organised a position for him in charge 'of foot' (infantry, 3.3.184); Falstaff wishes it had been 'of horse' (3.3.185). Hal is shifting into a leadership role, giving curt demands to Bardolph and Peto. There is now no time for frivolity: 'The land is burning, Percy stands on high' (3.3.200).

Key point

In 3.1, when the rebels use the map to divide the realm, Hotspur uses the word 'monstrous' (3.1.96) to express his view of the river reducing his share. Shakespeare intends his audience to think of the word as applicable to the rebels and Hotspur's proposal to redirect the river course. It suggests that what the rebels intend is unnatural. Glendower disputes Hotspur's ability to alter nature in this way. There is an implication that challenging the crown, despite the questions that hang over Henry IV's monarchy, is as unnatural, dangerous and 'monstrous' as rerouting a river course.

Key vocabulary

Induction (3.1.2): opening scene of a play

Lancaster (3.1.7): Henry IV

Cressets (3.1.13): metal baskets containing combustible material; flaming torches

Distemperature (3.1.31): disorder

In deep experiments (3.1.46): investigations into the occult

Made head (3.1.60): raised an army

Wye, Severn, Trent (3.1.61, 62, 75): rivers

Sealed interchangeably (3.1.77): so each party to the agreement has a copy signed by the other two

Moiety (3.1.92): share

Bottom (3.1.101): valley

Skimble-skamble (1.3.148): nonsense

Strange concealments (3.1.161): occult magic

Wanton (3.1.207): dispersed; rushes covering the floor

Doom (3.2.6): judgement

Pickthanks; newsmongers (3.2.25): taletellers

Skipping King (3.2.60): frivolous

Enfeoffed (3.2.69): surrendered

Wherefore (3.2.121): why

Vassal (3.2.124): base; abject

Knight of the Burning Lamp (3.3.27): a parody of a chivalric title; Falstaff means that Bardolph's face is bright red from drinking.

Memento mori (3.3.30): a reminder of death (usually a skull); Falstaff says that Bardolph's face will remind him of death.

Salamander (3.3.46): mythical lizard that could live in fire

Maid Marian (3.3.113): a character who had a reputation for being sexually promiscuous (presumably for associating with Robin Hood and his followers in the forest); Falstaff is insulting the Hostess by suggesting that the Hostess' reputation is worse than Maid Marian's.

Thing (3.3.114): female genitals

Lion (3.3.146): the lion was a symbol of royalty

Adam fell (3.3.163): According to the Bible, when Adam and Eve disobeyed God by eating from the tree of knowledge they were expelled from the garden of Eden and were thereafter mortal, subject to death. This event was termed the Fall because they 'fell' from God's grace.

With unwashed hands (3.3.182): quickly, without wasting time

Q What does Wales represent in the play and how does Shakespeare create such associations?

Q Analyse the confrontation between Henry IV and Hal in 3.2. What does the exchange reveal about their characters and the nature of kingship?

Act 4

4.1 Summary: *The rebels at Shrewsbury prepare for war. Prince Hal is transformed.*

A messenger arrives from Northumberland, advising that he cannot join the rebellion as he is sick; Hotspur is initially dismayed at the bad timing: 'This sickness doth infect / The very life-blood of our enterprise' (4.1.28–9). The rebels decide to continue, despite Worcester's doubts (4.1.60–75), and Hotspur is excited at the challenge of 'a larger dare' (4.1.78). Sir Richard Vernon arrives to tell them that Westmorland and Prince John (Hal's brother) are heading their way in support of the king.

Through Vernon's report we are presented with a new Hal. Hotspur's version of the prince as 'madcap' (4.1.95) is out of date. Vernon describes the prince and his comrades in mythic terms as 'like eagles' (4.1.99) 'glittering in golden coats' (4.1.100). Hal has a new name, 'young Harry' (4.1.104), and is 'gallantly armed' (4.1.105). He is compared to Mercury (4.1.106), the messenger of the classical gods, and transformed into a skilled horseman: he 'vaulted with such ease into his seat / As if an angel dropped down from the clouds / To turn and wind a fiery Pegasus, / And witch the world with noble horsemanship' (4.1.107–10). Hotspur is impatient for the battle to begin despite the further bad news that Glendower cannot join them for a fortnight: 'Doomsday is near. Die all, die merrily' (4.1.134).

4.2 Summary: *Falstaff confesses to misusing his position.*

Falstaff admits, in a soliloquy, that he has been corrupt in his position by accepting bribes from those wishing to avoid military service. The only soldiers Falstaff now has are those too poor to pay their way out – underfed, underdressed and ill-equipped for war. His unethical behaviour is consistent with his character, but in the context of war it evokes discomfort rather than humour.

4.3 Summary: *The rebels debate military tactics. Blunt arrives. The rebels outline their grievances against the king.*

The impatient Hotspur wants to press forward immediately but Worcester and Vernon urge him to wait until preparations are finalised. Sir Walter Blunt arrives. Loyal to the king, he sees the rebels' opposition as 'out of limit and true rule' for standing against 'anointed majesty' (4.3.39–40). On behalf of the king, he invites the rebels to state their grievances.

Hotspur replies that it was he and his family who *gave* Henry the crown (4.3.55). He suggests that Henry, when he returned from exile, came back only to be the Duke of Lancaster (4.3.61) not a king. The suggestion is that they only gave Henry assistance because he was aiming to recover the rank due to him. By aiming higher and obtaining the crown, Henry overreached himself and betrayed his promise. Hotspur claims it is Mortimer who should be the rightful king (4.3.93–5).

4.4 Summary: *The Archbishop gives letters to Sir Michael to deliver.*

The Archbishop suspects that Hotspur and the rebels will lose against the king; he reveals that Mortimer is not with the rebels.

Key point

In 4.2, Hal observes of Falstaff's soldiers 'I did never see such pitiful rascals' (4.2.62). Falstaff's response is callous: 'Tut, tut, good enough to toss, food for powder, food for powder, they'll fill a pit as well as better. Tush, man, mortal men, mortal men' (4.2.63–5). It is also morbidly accurate; in war, death will not distinguish between soldiers – by the end of the play the heroic Hotspur will be just as dead as Falstaff's miserable soldiers.

Key vocabulary

Stamp (4.1.4): stamping; coinage

Zounds (4.1.17): God's wounds (an oath)

Meet (4.1.33): appropriate

Feathered Mercury (4.1.106): Mercury was the messenger god, portrayed as having wings on both his cap and feet.

Pegasus (4.1.109): winged horse from classical mythology

The fire-eyed maid of smoky war (4.1.114): Bellona, Roman goddess of war

Mars (4.1.116): Roman god of war

Doomsday (4.1.134): judgement day; the end of the world

An angel (4.2.6): coin with the Archangel Michael stamped on it

Press (4.2.12): the process of forcing people to join the armies

Banns (4.2.17): public declaration of intended marriage

Caliver (4.2.19): light musket

Ancients (4.2.23): ensigns; flag-bearers

Revolted tapsters (4.2.28): runaway tavern employees

Prodigals (4.2.33): wastrels; from the biblical story of the prodigal son

Find linen enough on every hedge (4.2.46): linen was put out on hedges to dry; Falstaff is expecting them to steal clothing.

Vouchsafe (4.3.31): ensure

March (4.3.93): Mortimer

O'er-ruled by prophecies (4.4.18): suggesting Glendower didn't come because of adverse prophecies

Q Analyse Vernon's description of Hal in 4.1. How does he describe the prince and what is the effect?

Q What information do we get in this act about the plight of ordinary people forced to become soldiers in medieval times?

Act 5

5.1 Summary: *At Shrewsbury, the king and the rebels' representatives confront one another and the king makes a final offer of mercy. Falstaff contemplates the nature of honour.*

Henry's observation of the sun peering above the hill recalls Hal's earlier description of himself as a sun hidden by clouds, his virtue obscured (1.2.195–201). It anticipates Hal's imminent heroic glory. The king and prince are now acting in concert, not in conflict. Henry accuses Worcester and Vernon of deceiving his trust (5.1.11) and asks whether the rebels will become obedient again. Hal stifles Falstaff's attempts to chip in with a joke; this is no time for frivolity. Worcester admonishes the king for his ambition and betrayal of their support. He frames Henry's offence as a type of gluttony: 'Grew by our feeding to so great a bulk' (5.1.62), linking the king with Falstaff as a figure of excessive consumption.

Hal states that he admires Hotspur and proposes that they engage in single combat to avoid the battle. Henry gives the rebels one final chance to back down without penalty.

Falstaff mournfully expresses the life-threatening nature of war: 'I would 'twere bed-time, Hal, and all well' (5.1.125). His pragmatism challenges the ideal of honour that Hotspur and Hal seek. It is a sober questioning of war and the voice of the ordinary man contradicting the rhetoric that glorifies war.

5.2 Summary: *Worcester keeps the king's offer of mercy secret. Vernon describes the transformed prince and Hotspur rouses the troops for battle.*

Worcester decides not to communicate Henry's offer of mercy to the others, wanting the battle to proceed because he fears Henry will never trust them and therefore their lives will always be in danger: 'For treason is but trusted like the fox' (5.2.9). He lies to the others – 'There is no seeming mercy in the King' (5.2.34) – which demonstrates a lack of honesty within the rebel group. Hotspur is informed of Hal's challenge but rejects the idea. The transformed prince is described in glowing terms: 'modestly' (5.2.52), 'gentle' (5.2.54) and 'princely tongue' (5.2.56). Hotspur struggles to reconcile this description with what he knows of Hal, but resolves to defeat him and rouses the group to action: 'if we live, we live to tread on kings, If die, brave death when princes die with us!' (5.2.85–6).

5.3 Summary: *The battle ensues. Blunt, disguised as the king, is killed by Douglas. Hal chastises Falstaff for his lack of gravity on the battlefield.*

On a relatively small stage Shakespeare was unable to depict a battle in its entirety so his technique was to show short vignettes and interludes between fighting (which was implied to be happening offstage), or present single fights. Blunt enters disguised as the king. This was a common tactic to prevent the enemy from knowing the true king; it emphasises the theme of counterfeit royalty that runs throughout the play. Douglas kills Blunt, assuming he is the king.

Falstaff enters alone and fearful, observing to himself that almost all of his soldiers have been killed. Hal enters and chastises him for standing idle. When Hal discovers a bottle of wine in Falstaff's pistol case he is furious: 'What, is it a time to jest and dally now?' (5.3.55). Hal has adapted to the changed circumstances but Falstaff has remained the same.

5.4 Summary: *Prince Hal is now a military hero. He protects the king from Douglas and redeems his father's good opinion. He fights and kills Hotspur. Falstaff, in a fight with Douglas, falls down and pretends to be dead.*

Despite the king's advice to retire and see to his wounds, Hal resolves to keep fighting: 'God forbid a shallow scratch should drive / The Prince of Wales from such a field as this, / Where stained nobility lies trodden on, / And rebels' arms triumph in massacres!' (5.4.10–13). Hal's brother Lord John of Lancaster joins him – now father and both sons fight together in a show of Lancastrian solidarity. The sons exit and Douglas enters to find the real king. They fight, then Hal enters and proclaims his newly transformed identity: 'It is the Prince of Wales that threatens thee' (5.4.41). Hal has recovered his father's good opinion. Douglas flees and Hotspur enters.

This moment is the climax of the play, when the two rivals, Hal and Hotspur, finally come face to face. Hal boldly claims that he is not prepared to share honour and glory with Hotspur; he will take Hotspur's portion by defeating him (5.4.62–6). Falstaff enters and fights with Douglas before falling down and pretending to be dead. Falstaff's fight here is a parody of the honourable fight between Hal and Hotspur, providing a comic comparison. Hal kills Hotspur and, thinking Falstaff is dead, observes: 'I could have better spared a better man' (5.4.103); that is, Hal will miss him more than he would have missed a better man. Although Falstaff is not dead, the scene nevertheless registers the death of a friendship; from this point on Hal's relationship with the knight is irretrievably altered. Hal exits and Falstaff rises, reflecting, in a famous line, that 'The better part of valour is discretion, in the which better part I have saved my life' (5.4.118–19). Fearing that Hotspur, too, might be faking death (5.4.121), he resolves to make sure he is dead and pretend that he has killed him. Hal is surprised to see Falstaff alive and even further surprised to hear him claim he killed Hotspur. Hal knows that Falstaff is lying but, generously, is prepared to give Falstaff the credit for Hotspur's death. A trumpet signals that the king's forces have won.

5.5 Summary: *The king orders the execution of Worcester and Vernon. Hal shows mercy to Douglas. The royal forces have won the battle of Shrewsbury, quelling the rebellion for the moment.*

In the final scene Henry admonishes Worcester for not conveying his offer of mercy to the rebels and orders him, and Vernon, to be executed. Hal gains Henry's approval to deal with the captured Douglas and, significantly, shows mercy, a quality that many Shakespearean plays portray as important in leaders. Henry orders that John and Westmorland head to York to meet Northumberland and Scroop, who represent the rebels. Henry and Hal will head for Wales to fight Glendower and Mortimer. For the present the rebellion is quelled and Henry optimistically states: 'Rebellion in this land shall lose his sway' (5.5.41). The scene is set for the next play in the tetralogy, *2 Henry IV*.

Key point

In this act Shakespeare's figurative language gives a cosmic dimension to the battle. The king asks the rebels whether, to avoid war, they will 'move in that obedient orb again' (5.1.17) instead of being like 'an exhaled meteor' (5.1.19). The rebellion is likened to disorder in the cosmos. Likewise, when Hal confronts Hotspur he claims 'Two stars keep not their motion in one sphere, / Nor can one England brook a double reign / Of Harry Percy and the Prince of Wales' (5.4.64–6). Their rivalry is given a cosmic significance.

Key vocabulary

Distemperature (5.1.3): cosmic disorder

Seat of Gaunt (5.1.45): dukedom of John of Gaunt, Henry's father

Bestride (5.1.122): stand over

Colossus (5.1.123): a huge statue. The Colossus of Rhodes was one of the Seven Wonders of the ancient world.

Catechism (5.1.140): a question and answer technique that Falstaff has been using to explore the nature of honour

Marry (5.2.33): a mild oath – 'Mary' (not blasphemous)

Forswearing/forsworn (5.2.38): denying by a false oath

Gentle (5.2.54): noble (worthy of the nobility); graceful

Soft (5.3.32): wait

Ragamuffins (5.3.36): wretched soldiers

Peppered (5.3.36): killed

Grinning honour (5.3.59): grinning because you are dead (a skull); honour only through death

Hydra's heads (5.4.24): mythic monster with multiple heads – when one was cut off two more would grow in its place

Q Why does Worcester decide not to tell the other rebels of the king's offer of mercy?

Q What different perspectives on honour and military glory are presented in this act?

CHARACTERS & RELATIONSHIPS

In the medieval theatre that predated Shakespeare, characters had less depth and were generally embodiments of abstract ideas, such as vice, or figures known to the audience from biblical stories or historical tales. They fulfilled certain roles in a play, making it less important to provide detailed characterisation, since the characters were subservient to the overall structure of the play. Shakespeare is credited with being among the first playwrights to provide a greater interiority to his characters. By that, critics mean that he gives us more information about what the characters think and how they feel about events. We therefore construct a psychological profile for the characters. This depth is not provided uniformly across the characters; we learn more about some characters than others. There is also often complexity to Shakespeare's characters that makes us respond to them as plausible people rather than types (characters that represent certain ideas or embody particular human characteristics). Virtually none of Shakespeare's characters can be reduced to a simple stereotype; there are often flaws in his heroes and elements of virtue in his villains. At the same time, certain characters in *1 Henry IV* are indebted to earlier abstract figures; Falstaff is indebted to the Vice figure of the Morality Plays, and some critics view Hal as a type of 'everyman' having to choose the right way to live.

Henry IV

Key quotes

I know not whether God will have it so
For some displeasing service I have done,
That in his secret doom out of my blood
He'll breed revengement and a scourge for me ...
... Tell me else,
Could such inordinate and low desires,
Such poor, such bare, such lewd, such mean attempts,

Such barren pleasures, rude society,
As thou art matched withal, and grafted to,
Accompany the greatness of thy blood
And hold their level with thy princely heart? (3.2.4–7, 11–17)

Thou has redeemed thy lost opinion (5.4.47)

In *Richard II*, Henry Bolingbroke appears as young and energetic. In *1 Henry IV*, set shortly after, Henry seems to have aged with the burden of the crown. He is threatened by rebels, bears the weight of his conscience over the usurpation and death of Richard II and has the worry of his wayward son. The first lines of the play express the king's present state: 'So shaken as we are, so wan with care' (1.1.1).

Henry's low opinion of his son appears to be public knowledge. Hotspur accurately reflects: 'I think his father loves him not / And would be glad he met with some mischance' (1.3.228–9). This is a serious state of affairs; Hotspur discerns, with some justification, that the king's feelings are so negative towards his own son that he would be glad if Hal were dead. Henry sees the failings of his son as a form of punishment by God for his past deeds (3.2.4–11). By comparison, he cannot praise Hotspur enough, describing him as 'Mars in swaddling clothes' (3.2.112). Although threatened by Hotspur, Henry admires him. It is only in the final stages of the play that Henry sees his son in a new light, as Hal adopts the values important to his father.

Key point

At the end of the play-within-a-play, when Hal has been playing the king, Falstaff says: 'Never call a true piece of gold a counterfeit. Thou art essentially made without seeming so' (2.4.476–8). Falstaff is asking Hal to see him as something essentially 'true' and good, despite his outer appearance. Falstaff likens himself to Hal, as also having a 'true self' beneath his appearance. The observations, contrasting 'true' and 'counterfeit', invite comparison; is Henry IV a true or counterfeit king? What makes a real king – merit or inherited entitlement? The question becomes more complicated with Hal; he is inheriting the crown from his father, so it will be legitimately passed to him, but if Henry's right to the crown is questionable, does that taint Hal's succession? Henry's anxiety over Hal's behaviour and his concern that Hal appear and act as a 'true' heir to the throne is arguably grounded in these fears; with questions over their legitimacy, acting as a rightful monarch becomes even more important.

Prince Hal

Key quotes

I know you all, and will awhile uphold
The unyoked humour of your idleness.
Yet herein will I imitate the sun,
Who doth permit the base contagious clouds
To smother up his beauty from the world,
That when he please again to be himself,
Being wanted, he may be more wondered at
By breaking through the foul and ugly mists
Of vapours that did seem to strangle him.
If all the year were playing holidays,
To sport would be as tedious as to work;
But when they seldom come, they wished-for come,
And nothing pleaseth but rare accidents.
So when this loose behaviour I throw off, And pay the debt I never promisèd,
By how much better than my word I am,
By so much shall I falsify men's hopes.
And like bright metal on a sullen ground,
My reformation, glittering o'er my fault,
Shall show more goodly, and attract more eyes
Than that which hath no foil to set it off.
I'll so offend, to make offence a skill,
Redeeming time when men think least I will. (1.2.193–215)

Although Henry wishes that Hotspur were his son, rather than Hal, he underestimates the prince. At the end of the play it is Hotspur, with his uncompromising idealism and rash temperament, who will be dead. Hal is a survivor, an observer who adapts to his surroundings. He is able to move from the tavern to the battlefield, to associate with the ordinary people yet beat the most valiant of heroes.

To what extent is Hal part of the group of thieves that congregate in the tavern? Hal, in his speech with his companions, often includes himself as one of them (1.2.31). In 2.2 Hal seems to be an intimate part of the robbery, although he double-crosses his companions and repays the money. He is familiar with the language of the lower-class characters and with the slang terms of thieves, such as 'Lay by!', a robber's command (1.2.35). Hal is amused by Falstaff and enjoys the banter and trading of insults that constitute an important part of their relationship and manner of communication. These convey a complex mixture of both affection and derision. Hal, paradoxically, sees exactly what Falstaff is and yet has a true affection for him.

While Falstaff is ostensibly a bad influence on Hal, it is clear that the prince is intelligent and calculating. He is not easily led astray by anyone and appears in control of his own actions and capable of making his own decisions. At the end of 1.2 Hal foreshadows his future rejection of his companions and his reformation as a person. He compares himself to the sun allowing itself to be covered by clouds but eventually shining through. His statement 'I know you all' (1.2.193) suggests that the prince is not deluded by his tavern companions. Hal's argument is that, once he does reform and act in a way a prince is expected to act, his reformation will seem miraculous and his virtues and honour will seem all the greater by comparison with his present state. This makes his offences seem to be a strategic plan. It gives his character a cold, calculating dimension, often described as Machiavellian after the Italian political theorist Machiavelli (1469–1527).

The play-within-a-play in 2.4 demonstrates that Hal understands his father's concerns about him. At the same time, Hal's voice also comes through strongly. Hal's friendship with Falstaff does not preclude him from viewing the man critically; his tirade of insults (2.4.434–46) is as much Hal's voice as it is his playing the role of the king. In addition, this string of insults takes on a more sinister tone; references to the 'devil' (2.4.435), 'that reverend Vice' (2.4.441) and 'Satan' (2.4.450) add a moral and Christian condemnation. From the real king's perspective, what Hal is doing is not innocent fun: theft, drunkenness and lechery are sins, not just bad behaviour. They compromise the idea of the monarch as God's appointee and place the entire country at risk.

Key point

Hal predicts the change in his character ('when he please again to be himself', 1.2.198). This raises the question – what *is* the true character of the prince? Is he truly royal, temporarily pretending to be a thief, or will his new role, as virtuous prince, also just be an act? Is royalty and nobility simply a performance?

Sir John Falstaff

Key quotes

Banish plump Jack, and banish all the world. (2.4.465)

I was as virtuously given as a gentleman need to be. Virtuous enough. Swore little. Diced not above seven times a week. Went to a bawdy-house not above once in a quarter – of an hour. Paid money that I borrowed – three or four times. Lived well, and in good compass: and now I live out of all order, out of all compass. (3.3.14–20)

Falstaff is expansive, abundant and pleasure-seeking. He is also bold and daring in the way he treats Hal in a familiar, casual manner, calling him 'Hal' and 'lad'. He trusts that their friendship will continue to overcome the need for him to show excessive deference. Falstaff is a complex figure; on the one hand he is completely open about what he is ('we that take purses', 1.2.13–14); he does not try to hide from Hal his nature as a thief. On the other hand he is mired in layers of deceit; a teller of tall tales, Falstaff cannot tell a story without embellishment and without exaggeration. His very name evokes the word 'false'. He is a false and temporary father to Hal, false in his livelihood as a thief, false even to his fellow thieves, as Hal delightfully exposes. Yet there is something endearingly honest about him, a down-to-earth pragmatism that provides a welcome contrast to the intrigues of court. Hal can see through the layers of deceit and yet is able to love him. This love will, eventually, be compromised, displaced by the duties of Hal's future royal position, but early in *1 Henry IV* there is a genuine affection between the characters. Falstaff's affection for Hal is evident when he calls Hal 'the most comparative rascalliest sweet young prince' (1.2.80–1).

In 1.2 Falstaff jokes with Hal about 'when thou art King' (1.2.16). Although he jests throughout the play, this masks a genuine anxiety about how their relationship will change in the future. Falstaff comprehends that the nature of their friendship cannot be sustained once Hal wears the crown; the social gulf will be too great. His anxiety is clear when he asks Hal 'shall there be gallows standing in England when thou art King?' (1.2.58–9). He urges Hal 'Do not thou when thou art King hang a thief' (1.2.60–1), to which Hal retorts 'No, thou shalt' (1.2.62). He implies that Falstaff will hang (as a thief). Although it is a joke, it is also ominous. Falstaff misunderstands (or pretends to), saying that Hal will appoint him to the position of hangman (1.2.63–4).

Falstaff is the primary source of humour in the play. He is humorous when he criticises Hal for leading him astray: 'Thou hast done much harm upon me, Hal, God forgive thee for it' (1.2.91). This is comic because both characters and audience can see that Falstaff is the one ostensibly leading Hal astray; there is humour in Falstaff pretending that he is virtuous and that Hal is 'able to corrupt a saint' (1.2.91). When Falstaff says it is no sin 'for a man to labour in his vocation' (1.2.105) the humour lies in Falstaff's mock earnestness. He takes on the appearance and attitude of an honest labourer when, as a thief, he is no such thing and has no right to call stealing a 'vocation', which gives it the language of respectability.

In the play-within-a-play, Falstaff, playing the role of Hal, provides a different perspective of himself, defending his faults and pleading with Hal, as the king, to banish everyone except himself (2.4.419–20). When Falstaff says 'Banish plump Jack, and banish all the world' (2.4.465), he means that if Hal banishes Falstaff he rejects the world of ordinary people, for Falstaff embodies, albeit to excess, the ordinary foibles of human nature. Yet Hal answers him coldly and at no stage gives Falstaff the assurance he seeks.

Key point

Falstaff provides a contrast to the ideals of honour and heroism that Hotspur, and eventually Hal, display. Falstaff represents cowardice, which is both comic and at points endearingly human. When the thieves plan the robbery and Gadshill reports that there are eight or ten people, Falstaff panics, asking 'Zounds, will they not rob us?' (2.2.63). On the battlefield Falstaff is sceptical of honour and how it seems too closely connected with death, confirmed by the fact that Hotspur, for all his reputation, ends up dead.

Hotspur

Key quotes

> O, let the hours be short,
> Till fields, and blows, and groans applaud our sport! (1.3.296–7)
>
> He hath more worthy interest to the state
> Than thou the shadow of succession (3.2.98–9)
>
> Harry to Harry shall, hot horse to horse,
> Meet and ne'er part till one drop down a corpse (4.1.122–3)

Shakespeare made Hotspur about the same age as Hal in order to emphasise their rivalry and focus on the two characters as alternative models of young men. Hotspur is a gallant, militaristic young hero, admired wistfully by Henry IV, who wishes his own son were more like him. By altering Hotspur's age, Shakespeare creates dramatic energy. Hal's jealousy of Hotspur becomes a compelling motive for the transformation of Hal from tavern lout to noble prince and military hero. By defeating Hotspur, Hal wins the glory that was Hotspur's.

Hotspur seeks to define himself as a battle-hardened man of action. The appearance and behaviour of the king's foppish representative in 1.3 offends him. In criticising the other man, he defines himself as a man of practicality, not of appearance and refined sensibility; he is at home amid the blood and mire of the battlefield, not amid the preening fashions of court. Hotspur's short temper is also in evidence later when he is unwilling to listen to Worcester's attempts to counsel him to temper his wrath.

The rivalry between Hal and Hotspur is of central importance. Hotspur is derisive of the prince; he calls him 'that same sword-and-buckler Prince of Wales' (1.3.227). In the period in which the play is set, people judged others by the clothes they wore, their accessories and even their weapons. Hotspur is putting down his rival by suggesting that Hal uses a lower class of weaponry – implying he is not a true gentleman, let alone a prince, and so does not constitute a real threat. The nature of his threat, to 'have him poisoned with a pot of ale' (1.3.230) also reflects sarcastically on Hal's reputation.

Hotspur is blunt and direct and cannot abide flattery (4.1.6). He claims he does not have 'the gift of tongue' (5.2.77): 'For I profess not talking' (5.2.91). Compare this with Hal's claim of proficiency in language; he can easily learn the language of, and communicate with, the ordinary person (2.4.17–19). As a ruler this will be a valuable attribute for Hal; those like Hotspur, with no patience or interest in language differences, would struggle to unite the diverse places and people that make up the kingdom.

Key point

Hotspur and Hal function as different models of young men, both of whose behaviour is excessive. Prince Hal, initially, is too immoderate and irresponsible, while Hotspur, although courageous, is too rash and impetuous. The ideal behaviour for the young, heroic male, particularly a prince and future monarch, lies somewhere in between.

The minor characters

Glendower is described in the first scene as 'irregular and wild' (1.1.40). Wales was distinctly different from England in terms of its geography, language and culture and still retains its unique status. In Shakespeare's period, Wales, like Ireland, was thought of as a wild place, removed from the political centre and difficult for English monarchs to control. Cultural difference was generally seen as a threat. Glendower, as a Welshman, is seen as less civilised and of a lesser social status. He is described as having 'rude hands' (1.1.41). At the same time, he is also associated with magic and the mystery of Wales as a place of myth. Henry IV describes him as 'that great magician, damned Glendower' (1.3.82) and Hotspur describes Glendower's conversations about 'Merlin and his prophecies' and 'a dragon and a finless fish' (3.1.144–5). There is a dark side to these suggestions of magic; when Glendower says he can 'command the devil' (3.1.53) this suggests he dabbles in black magic.

Sir Walter Blunt is described in the first scene by the king as 'a dear, a true industrious friend' (1.1.62). He is reasonable and diplomatic: he supports Hotspur in 1.3, attempting to keep the peace between the king and Hotspur (to no avail). Although Blunt is on the king's side, the rebels also respect him and Hotspur expresses his admiration for him (4.3.32–7).

Worcester is also a figure of even temperament; in 1.3 he attempts to calm Hotspur and make him listen to reason. In 5.2 a more calculating side of Worcester emerges when he withholds the king's offer of mercy from the others lest they take it; he fears that the king will never trust them.

Douglas, a Scot, is another of the rebels, admired by Hotspur for his fighting prowess (5.3.14–15). Just as Glendower represents Wales, 'the Douglas' embodies Scotland. The Scots were renowned for their toughness in battle so when Prince Hal defeats Douglas at Shrewsbury, the transformation of Hal into a military hero is accentuated.

Mortimer is important because he represents a threat to Henry IV's throne. Shakespeare's character Edmund, Lord Mortimer, is a fusion of two historical persons named Edmund Mortimer. One was Hotspur's brother-in-law, the brother of his wife Elizabeth (who Shakespeare renames Kate in the play). This Edmund had a brother, Roger Mortimer, whose son was Edmund, Earl of March. Richard II had proclaimed the Earls of March (Roger, then his son Edmund) as his heirs. By confusing the two Edmunds, Shakespeare incorrectly calls Glendower's prisoner

Edmund (Hotspur's brother-in-law) the 'Earl of March' (1.3.83). In any event the historical Earl of March was loyal to Henry IV and Henry V (see Peter Davison's commentary in the 2005 Penguin edition, p.141).

Despite Hotspur trivialising his wife's concerns for him and ignoring her request to know what is going on, **Kate Percy** shows herself to be intelligent and perceptive; she guesses the reason for her husband's agitation: 'I fear my brother Mortimer doth stir / About his title, and hath sent for you / To line his enterprise' (2.3.84–6). Shakespeare also conveys the deep love between husband and wife.

A range of other minor characters helps to create the world of the play. **Mistress Quickly** is the hostess of the tavern in Eastcheap, enjoying the jovial conversation of Falstaff's circle and acting as a protective intermediary between the thieves and the authorities. **The Carriers** in 2.1 convey aspects of trade and the often difficult working conditions of ordinary people.

THEMES, IDEAS & VALUES

Unity and division

Key quotes

No more the thirsty entrance of this soil
Shall daub her lips with her own children's blood (1.1.5–6)

The edge of war, like an ill-sheathèd knife,
No more shall cut his master. (1.1.17–18)

Shakespeare's work explores ideas of unity and division. In the period in which the play is set, the United Kingdom did not exist. England, Scotland, Wales and Ireland were distinct territories and countries; the extent to which the monarch of England controlled these other territories was highly contested. When James I of England (who was already James VI of Scotland) succeeded to the English crown in 1603, he sought to unify Britain, however this did not happen in his lifetime.

A divided country was seen as weak and vulnerable to external threats, so internal conflict was something to be avoided. In the first scene Henry is faced with rebellion, which he must quash if he is to retain his crown and ensure the stability of England. In 3.1, the rebels plan how they will divide up England if they are successful. Shakespeare's audience, and any monarch, would have looked at this scene with a sense of horror. Many of Shakespeare's plays express the fear of division. In *King Lear*, division of the kingdom leads to tragedy. The destructive Wars of the Roses, the war between the Lancastrians and the Yorkists, was the theme of the first tetralogy Shakespeare wrote (*Henry VI Parts 1, 2* and *3*, and *Richard III*). The final play in that series, *Richard III*, sees the end of the Wars of the Roses with the defeat of Richard III at Bosworth Field by Henry Tudor, who becomes Henry VII, the first of the Tudors and grandfather of Elizabeth I. Henry VII married Elizabeth of York, thus uniting the two family houses and ending the civil conflict. Having completed that tetralogy, Shakespeare then went back in time to when the seeds of that conflict were sown, with *Richard II*. The threat of division and the destruction resulting from internal conflict is a theme that runs throughout both tetralogies.

Key point

Shakespeare conveys the way in which the group that usurped Richard II in order to support Henry Bolingbroke become Henry IV is inherently vulnerable to division because of human nature. As Worcester observes:

> The King will always think him in our debt,
> And think we think ourselves unsatisfied,
> Till he hath found a time to pay us home.
> And see already how he doth begin
> To make us strangers to his looks of love. (1.3.280–4)

Place

Key quote

> Where is he living, clipped in with the sea
> That chides the banks of England, Scotland, Wales,
> Which calls me pupil or hath read to me? (3.1.41–3)

I Henry IV conveys a strong sense of the different regions of Britain. In Shakespeare's time there was no elaborate scenery; the stage was reasonably bare and there would only have been a few simple props used. So how did Shakespeare create a grand epic sense of Britain and the different places and types of people within it? Through language. Even in the brief opening scene the imagination of the audience starts to create a mind map of the different localities, and the characters associated with those places who will interact and come into conflict in the play.

In the opening scene the king describes how Sir Walter Blunt 'new lighted from his horse' is 'Stained with the variation of each soil / Betwixt that Holmedon and this seat of ours' (1.1.63–5); the different soils convey the expanse of the kingdom and parallel the social and cultural differences in the kingdom. Similarly, Glendower gives a sense of the geography of Britain surrounded by sea (3.1.41–2). In 3.1 various landmark rivers are named: the Wye, the Severn and the Trent. Wales features strongly in the play as a wild space, peripheral to England. The Welsh are considered particularly barbaric and savage in war (1.1.41–6), beyond the 'civilised' rules of warfare. The Welsh are also associated with magic and the supernatural; this is particularly emphasised in 3.1.

Key point

Place is also bound up with language; 3.1 reminds the audience that differences in language, as much as place, created diversity within Britain.

Fathers and sons

Key quotes

A son who is the theme of honour's tongue,
Amongst a grove the very straightest plant,
Who is sweet Fortune's minion and her pride (1.1.80–2)

I will redeem all this on Percy's head,
And in the closing of some glorious day
Be bold to tell you that I am your son (3.2.132–4)

Throughout the play Shakespeare explores variations of father and son relationships, which suggest different ways of constructing masculinity. With regard to Henry IV and Hal, Henry has certain expectations of his son; he wants him to demonstrate a capacity for government and to develop a sense of responsibility. Initially, however, Hal shows little evidence of this. At the same time, Hotspur is the son Henry IV wishes he had; he acknowledges his 'envy' (1.1.78) of Lord Northumberland for having such a son. By comparison he only sees 'riot and dishonour stain the brow' (1.1.84) of his own son.

In the opening scene the king is openly admiring of the military exploits of Hotspur. He relates Hotspur's victory and how he has taken numerous prisoners: 'is not this an honourable spoil? / A gallant prize?'

(1.1.74–5). Westmorland's reply is: 'It is a conquest for a prince to boast of' (1.1.76). Hotspur is not a prince, yet he is compared to one; this suggests that actions and behaviours have the potential to create (or at least give the appearance of) royalty, rather than simply the possession of a title. This casual comment reflects on the position of the king, who made a conquest of the crown rather than inheriting it from Richard II. The king's admiration for Hotspur is swiftly turned to a source of sadness; Hotspur's prowess makes an unwelcome comparison with his own son, making Hal seem even less worthy.

Just as Hotspur is an alternative son to Henry, Falstaff is a father-figure to Hal, an alternative to the cold, stern Henry IV and the duties of court life. Falstaff shows Hal genuine affection – calling him 'sweet wag' (1.2.16) – and presents a very different approach to life. Falstaff is able to hone Hal's skills in speech as they engage in verbal sparring. Teasing wordplay expresses affection and cements their bond of friendship. Hal does not receive this from his father. Although Falstaff is a self-centred opportunist, his pragmatism teaches Hal something, even though Hal scorns him. Through Falstaff, Hal learns to be an ordinary person. This will be an important lesson for when Hal becomes an extraordinary person, a monarch.

Key point

In 5.4 Hal finally redeems himself in the eyes of his father. He excels pursuant to the values his father places weight on – military prowess and courage. When he challenges Douglas and protects his father, Hal proclaims his new identity and role: 'It is the Prince of Wales that threatens thee, / Who never promiseth but he means to pay.' (5.4.41–2)

Succession

Key quotes

... drove us to seek out
This head of safety, and withal to pry
Into his title, the which we find
Too indirect for long continuance. (4.3.102–5)

I fear thou art another counterfeit,
And yet, in faith, thou bearest thee like a king – (5.4.34–5)

In late sixteenth century England, the issue of succession was of great concern, since Elizabeth I had no children and had not named an heir. Without a smooth transition of power the kingdom was vulnerable to chaos and conflict. *1 Henry IV* reflects these anxieties and demonstrates that holding on to the crown is not assured; rather, possession of the crown seems particularly fragile. Henry, having wrested the crown from Richard in the previous play, knows all too well how tenuous the hold on the crown can be. Since he himself did not respect the traditional rules of royal succession, it cannot be guaranteed that his subjects will respect the future succession of the crown by Prince Hal. Holding on to the crown now depends to some extent on the loyalty of the monarch's subjects and the earning of their respect. That Falstaff engages in thievery creates a subtle link to the larger idea that haunts *1 Henry IV* – that Henry IV is a thief on a grander scale, having taken the crown from Richard II. Shakespeare thus subtly suggests connections between the upper and lower sectors of society, with each reflecting the other.

Key point

The theme of illegitimacy pervades the play, surfacing in different ways. In 5.4 when Douglas, having already killed Blunt dressed as the king, finds the real king, he asks 'What art thou / That counterfeitest the person of a king?' (5.4.26–7). Although Douglas refers to the king's clothing, the question challenges Henry's legitimacy, an issue that has haunted him from the opening scene of the play. Yet Douglas' observation that he 'bearest thee like a king' (5.4.35) suggests a king can be recognised by his bearing and is thus more than superficial clothing.

Honour

Key quotes

By heaven, methinks it were an easy leap
To pluck bright honour from the pale-faced moon,
Or dive into the bottom of the deep,
Where fathom-line could never touch the ground,
And pluck up drownèd honour by the locks,
So he that doth redeem her thence might wear
Without corrival all her dignities.
But out upon this half-faced fellowship! (1.3.199–206)

Can honour set to a leg? No. Or an arm? No. Or take away the grief of a wound? No. Honour hath no skill in surgery then? No. What is honour? A word. What is in that word honour? What is that honour? Air. A trim reckoning! Who hath it? He that died a'Wednesday. Doth he feel it? No. Doth he hear it? No. 'Tis insensible, then? Yea, to the dead. But will it not live with the living? No. Why? Detraction will not suffer it. Therefore I'll none of it. Honour is a mere scutcheon – and so ends my catechism. (5.1.131–40)

Is honour something that should be sought? Throughout the play different characters reflect on this question. Hotspur speaks of honour in hyperbolic terms, wanting it all to himself (1.3.199–206). By comparison, Falstaff is much more sceptical; he questions honour in an important speech that contrasts the ephemeral nature of honour with the greater value of being alive (5.1.129–40). After Sir Walter Blunt is killed, Falstaff observes: 'I like not such grinning honour as Sir Walter hath' (5.3.58–9). This is in stark contrast to Hotspur who laments the honour Hal has won of him, 'those proud titles' (5.4.78), more than the loss of life itself.

Hal's position on honour shifts over the course of the play. In the beginning, he appears not to care that his honour and reputation are in jeopardy due to his behaviour and his associates. Gradually, however, he begins to care about honour and is envious of Hotspur, for his public reputation and the high esteem that King Henry has for him. Hal, in the climactic battle, defeats Hotspur and, in doing so, is cognisant that he takes from Hotspur all the honour that had previously accrued to the military hero.

DIFFERENT INTERPRETATIONS

Different interpretations arise from different responses to a text. Over time, a text will evoke a wide range of responses from its readers, who may come from various social or cultural groups and live in very different places and historical periods. These responses can be published in newspapers, journals and books by critics and reviewers, or they can be expressed in discussions among readers in the media, classrooms, book groups and so on. While there is no single correct reading or interpretation of a text, it is important to understand that an interpretation is more than a personal opinion – it is the justification of a point of view on the text. To present an interpretation of the text based on your point of view you must use a logical argument and support it with relevant evidence from the text.

The critics' viewpoints

Literary criticism, often referred to as 'secondary sources', is writing *about* a text, the 'primary source'. Literary criticism analyses, comments on and offers a particular interpretation of the primary text. Literary critics, in writing about a text, are entering into a dialogue with other critics and so try to take into account the opinions of others. Since Shakespeare's work has been around a long time, there is a substantial amount of critical material about his plays and poetry. This can be daunting for students and critics alike. Whether you are expected to research some literary criticism as part of your study of the play will depend on your level and the expectations of your teacher. If you do need to consider this, keep in mind that it is not possible for anyone to read and understand everything that is relevant to the play. Try to select a few articles or book sections that discuss an area of interest to you. Reading literary criticism should be enjoyable and is intended to help you order your thoughts and shape your own ideas about the play. It can also open your eyes to aspects of the play that you hadn't noticed.

As well as literary criticism, different interpretations of the play are made every time it is performed as a stage production or produced as a film. A particular production constitutes an interpretation because directors, script editors, cinematographers and others make choices to cut, add or rearrange lines and scenes. Choices are also made regarding costumes, sets, casting, props, music, sound and visual effects, all of which are aspects that allow varying interpretations of the play. Audiences will bring their own experiences to the play and respond to it in subjective ways. Enhance your reading of criticism by viewing some film and television versions of *1 Henry IV* and the other plays in the tetralogy: *Richard II*, *2 Henry IV* and *Henry V*. Watching all four plays will give you a sense of the series, common themes and how characters change in different plays.

If you are new to Shakespeare it is useful to start with background information about his life, historical period and why he has proved to be such an enduring writer. Some excellent places to start are: Jonathan Bate's *Soul of the Age* (2008), his earlier work *The Genius of Shakespeare* (1997), Stephen Greenblatt's *Will in the World: how Shakespeare became Shakespeare* (2004) and Peter Ackroyd's *Shakespeare: The Biography* (2005). Also very useful are *The Oxford Companion to Shakespeare* (2001), with plot summaries and valuable critical and stage histories on each of the plays, and *The Shakespeare Encyclopedia* (2009) which is useful as a general introduction, and for a wealth of images from the early modern period and from stage and film productions. *The Cambridge Companion to Shakespeare* (2001) is also an invaluable resource with essays by different contributors on Shakespeare's life, what he read, his language, genres, portrayal of gender, and the life of the theatre in Shakespeare's time.

In terms of approaching *1 Henry IV* from the perspective of genre, some valuable insights can be found in Warren Chernaik's *The Cambridge Introduction to Shakespeare's History Plays* (2007) and *The Cambridge Companion to Shakespeare's History Plays* (2002). These will help you to think about aspects relevant to *1 Henry IV* as well as issues common to all of Shakespeare's history plays.

Many scholarly editions of the play provide a valuable introduction and overview, considering themes, historical contexts and aspects of characterisation; they provide summaries of the different approaches taken by critics and look at stage and film histories. These can provide a useful starting point for determining which aspects of the play you wish to research. Charles Edelman has a comprehensive introduction to the Penguin edition (2005). Also look at the excellent introductions to the New Cambridge, Arden and Oxford editions of the play, and the Oxford School Shakespeare series by Oxford University Press (*1 Henry IV* 2008) aimed at secondary school students. It is also useful to look at edited collections of essays on the play, which provide a range of different perspectives, rather than just one critic's viewpoint. An example is *Henry the Fourth, Part I and II: Critical Essays* (1986) edited by David Bevington.

1 Henry IV raises various issues that have been explored throughout its critical history, such as the relationship between Hal and Falstaff, Falstaff and the king as alternative father-figures, issues surrounding the crown and succession, the relationship between the play and historical sources, language, historical contexts such as England's embattled colonisation of Ireland, representations of place and social classes in the play and many other significant topics. In seeking an overview of the diverse issues that the play raises, two excellent starting places are Marjorie Garber's chapter on the play in her *Shakespeare After All* (2004), and Jean Howard's introduction to the play in *The Norton Shakespeare* (2nd edn, 2008).

When using the internet for research, aim for peer-reviewed sites. An invaluable place to start for *1 Henry IV* is the Internet Shakespeare Editions series (http://internetshakespeare.uvic.ca/Foyer/plays/1H4.html).

This has a wealth of useful information on the play including introductory essays, with an in-depth outline of the play's critical reception, historical information and images, questions that the play raises and information on previous stage productions.

Once you are ready for a further challenge, *The Henriad* (2008), in the *Shakespeare on Screen* series, is a collection of essays on different film versions of *1 Henry IV* and the other plays in the tetralogy; it includes a comprehensive list of the various film versions made up to 2008.

Two contrasting interpretations

Any text is open to contrasting, yet equally valid, interpretations. Here are two different arguments on the political conflict in the play.

1. *1 Henry IV* continually emphasises the king's illegitimacy and suggests that the earlier usurpation, related in *Richard II*, was wrong.

Throughout the play there are serious questions over Henry IV's right to the crown. In the opening scene he announces plans to go on a holy pilgrimage, which evidences his guilt over his usurpation of the crown from Richard II and Richard II's death. He sees the burden of Hal's waywardness as God's revenge for his past deeds, presumably for the taking of the crown. The basis of a monarch's legitimacy is a central issue in the play. When Henry instructs Hal on how to behave in appropriate ways as a monarch, Henry seems particularly sensitive to the need to appear like a monarch. Implicitly this suggests that, where there are questions over the legitimacy of a monarch, the need to appear regal becomes more important.

The theme of illegitimacy is also alluded to in subtle ways throughout the play by parallels with the tavern plot. The robbing of the robbers, by Hal and Poins of Falstaff and friends, has an implicit parallel in the rebellion against the king. The implication is that just as Henry IV stole the crown from Richard II, he now faces the threat of the crown being taken from him.

The sin of pride could likewise be levelled at Henry. The rebels have a legitimate argument when they outline their complaints at Shrewsbury. When he was Henry Bolingbroke, wrongfully deprived of his estates, the rebels were prepared to help him recover his rightful ownership of the Dukedom of Lancaster. However, Henry went further by claiming the crown. The language of the play suggests a lack of moderation in this regard, linking Henry to Falstaff as a figure of excess. At the battle of Shrewsbury when Douglas confronts the real king, he asks whether the king is a counterfeit, a question that strikes at the heart of Henry IV's reign.

2. The play is sympathetic to Henry IV and casts the rebels in a negative light.

Shakespeare was adept at seeing situations from multiple perspectives and presenting both positive and negative aspects of his characters for audiences to consider. While there are, throughout the play, suggestions that Henry IV's legitimacy as a monarch is open to question, the play casts the rebels in a negative light, suggesting that they do not represent viable alternatives and that a strong central government, irrespective of the doubts that hang over Henry's crown, is preferable to the disunity and division that the rebels represent.

In 3.1 the audience is presented with a scene where the rebels use a map to plan the future division of the country. Maps were a powerful political tool in the early modern period, particularly valuable to those wanting to exercise power and control over people and places. The map here is emblematic of the country – what the rebels plan in terms of the symbolic space of the map will be enacted on the real landscape of the kingdom. The scene depicts a future of division, not unity, and would have been viewed by Shakespeare's audience with alarm. Internal divisions not only represented a risk to stable government but also rendered the country vulnerable to external attack. Thus the association of the rebels with disunity and division strongly suggests that they are to be viewed in a negative light.

The rebels are presented as a disparate and disunited group. Northumberland is sick and unable to join them; Glendower fails to show up (perhaps in accordance with prophecies predicting failure of the enterprise) and likewise Mortimer, the alternative heir to the throne, doesn't arrive. The rebels are depicted going into battle only half-ready, and as a divided group. Moreover, there is a lack of trust within the group. Worcester keeps the king's offer of mercy from the others. There is also a lack of respect for differences; Hotspur is not interested in or respectful of the Welsh. Furthermore, his arrogant claim that he will reroute a river connotes the sin of pride, and suggests that the rebels' plans are unnatural and, likewise, that their challenge to the king is unnatural.

The rebels are also depicted negatively through the personal attributes of their leader. Hotspur is depicted as rash and impatient. He has no diplomatic skills, no patience with Glendower and doesn't listen to the advice and counsel of his colleagues. He is often chastised by others for not listening to differing views and acting without caution. He rushes into battle against the advice of his fellow rebels, not waiting until the horses are ready and the rest of the forces arrive. The fact that he is accused of a 'want of government' suggests a man who, unable to govern himself, would not make a good leader. This taints the whole rebel faction.

QUESTIONS & ANSWERS

This section focuses on your own analytical writing on the text, and gives you strategies for producing high quality responses in your coursework and exam essays.

Essay writing – an overview

An essay is a formal and serious piece of writing that presents your point of view on the text, usually in response to a given essay topic. Your 'point of view' in an essay is your interpretation of the meaning of the text's language, structure, characters, situations and events, supported by detailed analysis of textual evidence.

Analyse – don't summarise

In your essays it is important to avoid simply summarising what happens in a text:

- A **summary** is a description or paraphrase (retelling in different words) of the characters and events. For example: 'Macbeth has a horrifying vision of a dagger dripping with blood before he goes to murder King Duncan'.
- An **analysis** is an explanation of the real meaning or significance that lies 'beneath' the text's words (and images, for a film). For example: 'Macbeth's vision of a bloody dagger shows how deeply uneasy he is about the violent act he is contemplating – as well as his sense that supernatural forces are impelling him to act'.

A limited amount of summary is sometimes necessary to let your reader know which part of the text you wish to discuss. However, always keep this to a minimum and follow it immediately with your analysis (explanation) of what this part of the text is really telling us.

Plan your essay

Carefully plan your essay so that you have a clear idea of what you are going to say. The plan ensures that your ideas flow logically, that your argument remains consistent and that you stay on the topic. An essay plan should be a list of **brief dot points** covering no more than half a page.

- Include your central argument or main contention – a concise statement of your overall response to the topic.
- Write three or four dot points for each paragraph, indicating the main idea and evidence/examples from the text. Note that in your essay you will need to *expand* on these points and *analyse* the evidence.

Structure your essay

An essay is a complete, self-contained piece of writing. It has a clear beginning (the introduction), middle (several body paragraphs) and end (the last paragraph or conclusion). It must also have a central argument that runs throughout, linking each paragraph to form a coherent whole. See examples of introductions and conclusions in the 'Sample analysis of a topic' and 'Sample answer' sections.

The introduction establishes your overall response to the topic. It includes your main contention and outlines the main evidence you will refer to in the course of the essay. Write your introduction after you have done a plan and before you write the rest of the essay.

The body paragraphs argue your case – they present evidence from the text and explain how this evidence supports your argument. Each body paragraph needs:

- a strong **topic sentence** (usually the first sentence) that states the main point being made in the paragraph
- **evidence** from the text, including some brief quotations
- **analysis** of the textual evidence, with **explanation** of its significance and how it supports your argument
- **links back to the topic** in one or more statements, usually towards the end of the paragraph.

Connect the body paragraphs so that your discussion flows smoothly. Use some linking words and phrases like 'similarly' and 'on the other hand', though don't start every paragraph like this. Another strategy is to use a significant word from the last sentence of one paragraph in the first sentence of the next.

Use key terms from the topic – or synonyms for them – throughout, so the relevance of your discussion to the topic is always clear.

The conclusion ties everything together and finishes the essay. It includes strong statements that emphasise your central argument and provide a clear response to the topic.

Avoid simply restating the points made earlier in the essay – this will end on a very flat note and imply that you have run out of ideas and vocabulary. The conclusion is meant to be a logical extension of what you have written, not just a repetition or summary of it. Writing an effective conclusion can be a challenge. Try using these tips:

- Start by linking back to the final sentence of the second-last paragraph, rather than just leaping back to your main contention straight away – this helps your writing to flow.
- Use synonyms and expressions with equivalent meanings to vary your vocabulary. This allows you to reinforce your line of argument without being repetitive.
- When planning your essay, think of one or two broad statements or observations about the text's wider meaning. These should be related to the topic and your overall argument. Keep them for the conclusion, since they will give you something 'new' to say but still follow logically from your discussion. The introduction will be focused on the topic, but the conclusion can present a wider view of the text.

Essay topics

1 Discuss the relationship between Prince Hal and Falstaff. What are the positive and negative aspects of it and how do these affect events in the play?

2 *1 Henry IV* is a history play. What is the nature of this genre and why do you think it was so popular with Shakespeare's audience?

3 What is the function and significance of the play-within-a-play in 2.4?

4 In *1 Henry IV* what associations are evoked in relation to the different places and how does place affect characterisation?

5 *1 Henry IV* raises various questions about the nature of the crown and who is entitled to the burden and power of it. Discuss.

6 Prince Hal is seen as undergoing a transformation in character over the course of the play. How does Shakespeare express and convey this process?

7 Discuss the importance of language in *1 Henry IV*; how does Shakespeare use language in different ways to convey aspects of the narrative, characters or themes in the play?

8 The historical figure of Hotspur was much older than Prince Hal. Why do you think Shakespeare made Hotspur of a similar age to the prince and what is the effect of this in the play?

9 How is the world of ordinary, lower-class people conveyed in the play? What different aspects of their lives do you think Shakespeare was interested in and what is the dramatic effect and function of these in the play?

10 Falstaff is one of Shakespeare's most popular and well-known characters. Why do you think this is so?

Useful vocabulary for writing on *1 Henry IV*

Below is a list of words you might find useful when writing about the play and literary or dramatic works generally. Also note that when you refer to a line from the play you will generally be asked to use numbers that refer to the act, scene and line. For example, a reference 2.4.10 means Act 2 Scene 4, line 10.

Act: major division in a play. In *1 Henry IV* there are five acts.

Blank verse: plain verse with no rhyming words at the end of the lines.

Character: fictional person in a literary or dramatic work.

Dramatic irony: when the audience knows something of which a character is unaware.

Early modern period: the early modern period is generally 1500–1800.

Elizabethan: refers to the period in which Elizabeth I was on the throne (1558–1603). Plays written after her death in 1603, when James I became king, fall into the Jacobean period.

Foreshadowing: an idea, event or imagery within a literary or dramatic work that anticipates an event that will occur later in the narrative.

Genre: a category of literary or dramatic works with a set of conventions (rules) about the characteristics of that type of work. Examples are comedy, tragedy and history.

Henriad: Shakespeare's second tetralogy, consisting of *Richard II*, *Henry IV Parts 1 & 2*, and *Henry V*.

Historical context: aspects of the society and culture of the period and the place in which a text was produced that may be relevant to take into account when reading the play and that will assist in understanding it. This may include events, attitudes, other texts, behaviours, objects, beliefs and values.

Iambic pentameter: where a line of verse has the stresses (beats) falling on every second syllable (iambic), and there are five stresses to a line (pentameter), totalling ten syllables.

Medieval: generally refers to the period 500–1500.

Metadramatic and Metatheatrical: reflective of the function and process of drama and the theatre itself. The play-within-a-play is metadramatic and metatheatrical because it reminds the audience they are watching a play and invites them to think about what drama is.

Metaphor: word or phrase used to describe something else by way of direct comparison. The word comes from a Greek term meaning 'carrying from one place to another'.

Oxymoron: contradictory terms used in conjunction.

Personification: figure of speech where an abstract idea, animal or inanimate object is given human characteristics.

Prose: speech or written language that is plain, not patterned, appearing like ordinary sentences in conversation. The word comes from the Latin word *prosa* meaning 'straightforward discourse'. You will recognise it in the play when the sentences continue to the edge of the page.

Renaissance: in relation to English literature, the period from the late 1500s up until 1660. Shakespeare was writing in the English Renaissance period.

Rhyming couplet: two lines of verse, the last words of which rhyme.

Scene: a subdivision of an act in a play. It also describes the visual appearance of the space in which the action is located. The word 'scene' derives from a Greek word that originally referred to the tent or booth behind the stage area in which the actors would get changed. Eventually the outside of the structure was decorated to fit in with the drama, leading to the idea of 'scenery'. (Note, however, there was very little stage scenery or props used in original Shakespearean theatre.)

Simile: similar to a metaphor but using the words 'as' or 'like'; for example, 'Such as is bent on sun-like majesty' (3.2.79).

Soliloquy: a dramatic speech spoken by a single character, usually when alone on stage.

Sonnet: verse comprised of fourteen lines with a specific rhyming pattern (rhyming couplets or other combinations).

Stage direction: note in the text of a play that tells actors what to do. These are generally minimal in the Elizabethan and Jacobean periods.

Tetralogy: a series of four related plays. Shakespeare wrote two tetralogies.

Verse: a line of metrical writing. The word 'meter' comes from the Greek word for 'measure' and refers to a pattern of stressed and unstressed syllables. You can often identify it in the play when you see that a character's speech lines don't continue to the edge of the page. Verse lines are structured and shaped into particular patterns. In Shakespeare's plays the verse is in iambic pentameter and often uses rhyme. (The word 'verse' can also refer to a stanza, which is a paragraph in a poem, and to poetry in general.)

Sample analysis of a topic

Falstaff is one of Shakespeare's most popular and well-known characters. Why do you think this is so?

Sample introduction

The character of Falstaff in *1 Henry IV* (1596) is one of Shakespeare's most memorable and well-loved characters. Audiences respond to him for a variety of reasons and while they, like Prince Hal, are able to discern his faults, it is precisely these failings that create our attraction to him. This essay will analyse the different facets of the character, and argue that his vices, comic wit and role as an alternative father-figure to Hal render him central to the play and are primary reasons for the play's popularity.

Paragraph outline

Body paragraph 1:

Topic sentence: Falstaff is a figure of excess and a model of intemperance. It would be useful to start with the idea of the Seven Deadly Sins and the idea of temperance as an ideal of behaviour in Shakespeare's period. This gives your reader some historical context to the depiction of Falstaff's behaviour. Find examples and some representative quotations from the play of Falstaff's vices: how he eats and drinks to excess, gambles, steals and spends his time in the tavern. Then conclude with some observations on how Falstaff provides one alternative to Hal, albeit a poor model, of how the prince can behave and spend his time.

Body paragraph 2:

Topic sentence: If Falstaff embodies a range of human failings, why does Hal have a close relationship with him, and why is he so appealing to an audience? Here you can analyse the way in which Falstaff seems to provide an alternative father-figure to Hal; whereas Henry IV is distant and disapproving of his son, Falstaff shows genuine affection for the prince. Find examples in the play that contrast how Falstaff and the king behave towards Hal. Also think about how Falstaff treats the prince in a familiar way, thus allowing him to be an ordinary person; look closely at the language Falstaff uses. Conclude the paragraph with some observations on how Falstaff also appeals to us because we, the audience, can see aspects of our own faults in him. We can relate to him as a fallible human being.

Body paragraph 3:

Topic sentence: Central to the comic appeal of Falstaff is his inability to tell the truth and his hypocrisy. There are many useful examples you could draw from in this paragraph. Look at the scene where Falstaff lies to Hal about fighting off the 'robbers' and how, when confronted with the truth, he has to concoct the further lie that he knew all along it was

Hal. Also think about his complaints in 2.4 of society's 'roguery', and how he fails to see himself as anything other than virtuous. Make some observations about why this works well as comedy and how Hal, and the audience, enjoy Falstaff's untruths.

Body paragraph 4:

Topic sentence: In the latter part of the play the darker side of Falstaff is revealed and the audience begins to understand why Hal, in becoming a king, will have to reject his friend. In this paragraph you need to outline the more sinister side of Falstaff. Look for examples of how he behaves in war and think about the king's confrontation with his son. Outline the qualities that Hal must exhibit as a king and why a friendship with Falstaff is incompatible with the prince's royal role. At the same time you might want to think about the implicit parallels between Falstaff, as a thief, and Henry IV, as a 'thief' of the crown.

Sample conclusion

> To conclude, Falstaff is a complex and intriguing character. His vices are a source of immense comedy and allow us to relate to the character. Like Hal we see through his lies and exaggerated tales and are drawn to him in any event. Falstaff functions as both an alternative father-figure to the prince and one example of how the prince can choose to act in life. At the same time, there is a darker side to the character that becomes more emphasised in the latter part of the play. Like Hal, we come to realise that, despite our love for Falstaff, the friendship can only be temporary; Falstaff's behaviour does not represent a viable way of life for a future monarch. Yet the impact and appeal of the character are such that, when the rejection comes in *2 Henry IV*, we will feel immense sorrow for the fall of the exuberant rogue.

SAMPLE ANSWER

What is the function and significance of the play-within-a-play in 2.4?

In *1 Henry IV* (1596) Shakespeare uses the device of a play-within-a-play in 2.4. Falstaff plays the role of the king, Henry IV, and Hal plays himself, in order to practise the imminent confrontation Hal will have with his father over his wayward behaviour and friendship with Falstaff. Then they swap roles; Hal plays the king and Falstaff plays Hal. This essay will explore the play-within-a-play device and argue that it enables both characters to explore different perspectives and express the underlying tensions and problematic nature of their friendship. The device also invites the audience to reflect on the theme of role-playing generally within the play.

When Falstaff plays the king, it enables him to articulate various perspectives on his friendship with Hal. He firstly expresses the views of Henry IV, which both Falstaff and Hal know to be highly critical of their friendship: 'Shall the son of England prove a thief, and take purses?' (2.4.402). Here Falstaff expresses both the dismay of the king that the prince's company 'doth defile' him (2.4.406), but also Falstaff's personal hope that Hal will remain close to him. Falstaff is also able to express his own deep, underlying fears about the future; how will Hal treat him once Hal is king and what will happen to their friendship? In playing the king, Falstaff's own voice also comes clearly through; he plays an advocate, using words such as 'goodly' (2.4.412), 'pleasing', and 'noble' (2.4.413). He pleads for the future king, Hal, not to reject him: 'Him keep with, the rest banish' (2.4.419–20). Multiple voices thus emerge from the role playing. Shakespeare's device is also a significant vehicle for Hal to realise the problems created by his relationship with Falstaff, despite his companion's appeal and the genuine affection between the two. By taking on the role of the current king, Henry IV, Hal is forced to contemplate his future role as a king and to see Falstaff from a monarch's perspective. This confirms the view that he has already expressed earlier in the play, that his friendship with a thieving, lying man, who spends his life in the tavern, cannot continue indefinitely and is incompatible with the role expected of a monarch. Acting the role of king in this play can be seen as an important step in Hal's progression towards reform. When he says coldly to Falstaff 'I do, I will' (2.4.466), it recalls his earlier 'I know you all' speech (1.2.193–215). It also anticipates the change in Hal's behaviour that we see come to fruition in Act 3 and foreshadows Hal's ultimate rejection of Falstaff, which will occur in *2 Henry IV*.

The play-within-a-play also explores the border between monarchs and ordinary people and invites the audience to reflect on the nature of kingship. How should a king act? What behaviour is befitting a monarch: being distant from or mixing with the ordinary people? Hal realises that a monarch cannot be of the world; he must banish the ordinary world in order to play the superhuman role of God's appointee. Through Falstaff playing the king, Shakespeare also draws the audience's attention to the way in which Falstaff is an alternative father-figure to Hal. Henry IV and Falstaff provide different mentoring skills and alternative behaviour for Hal to follow; one represents an austere commitment to duty while the other embodies disorder and excess. Hal must then choose what kind of values he will embody and what kind of monarch he will be.

The device of a play-within-a-play is a significant moment in *1 Henry IV* that brings to the surface the underlying tensions in Falstaff and Hal's friendship, and enables the characters to explore different roles and points-of-view. It explores the questions surrounding the role of a monarch, and the nature of royalty as a role to be performed, and foreshadows Hal's ultimate rejection of his friend. Shakespeare's device is also metadramatic, reminding those in the audience that they are watching a play in which actors pretend to be kings and princes. The device invites the audience to think about the way drama enables us to explore different perspectives and ideas relevant to our lives. Overall, the play-within-a-play creates a significant and intriguing moment in *1 Henry IV*.

REFERENCES & READING

Text

Davison, P (ed.) 2005, *William Shakespeare Henry IV, Part 1*, Penguin Books, London. (All quotations and most of the glossary have been drawn from the Penguin edition.)

References

Ackroyd, P 2005, *Shakespeare: The Biography*, Vintage, London.

Bate, J 2008, *Soul of the Age*, Penguin, London.

——1997, *The Genius of Shakespeare*, Picador, London.

Bevington, D 1986, *Henry the Fourth, Parts I and II: Critical Essays*, Garland Press, New York.

Chernaik, W 2007, *The Cambridge Introduction to Shakespeare's History Plays*, Cambridge University Press, Cambridge.

Cohen, W, Greenblatt, S, Howard, JE & Eisaman Maus, K (eds) 1997, *The Norton Shakespeare*, WW Norton & Company, New York and London.

De Grazia, M & Wells, S (eds) 2001, *The Cambridge Companion to Shakespeare*, Cambridge University Press, Cambridge.

Dobson, M & Wells, S (eds) 2001, *The Oxford Companion to Shakespeare*, Oxford University Press, Oxford.

Driver, E, Forbes, S, Mapps, J & Trewby, M (eds) 2009, *The Shakespeare Encyclopedia*, Global Book Publishing, Sydney.

Garber, M 2004, *Shakespeare after All*, Anchor Books, New York; Toronto.

Gill, R (ed.) 2008, *Henry IV Part 1 (Oxford School Shakespeare Series)*, Oxford University Press, Oxford.

Greenblatt, S 2004, *Will in the World: How Shakespeare Became Shakespeare*, Pimlico, London.

Hatchuel, S & Vienne-Guerrin, N (eds) 2008, *Shakespeare on Screen: The Henriad*, Publications des Universites de Rouen et du Havre, Rouen.

Hattaway, M (ed.) 2002, *The Cambridge Companion to Shakespeare's History Plays*, Cambridge University Press, Cambridge.

Kastan, DS (ed.) 1999, *A Companion to Shakespeare*, Blackwell, Oxford.

——2002, *King 1 Henry IV*, Arden Shakespeare, Third Series, London.

Kermode, F 2001, *Shakespeare's Language*, Penguin, London.

Weil, H & Weil, J (eds) 2008, *First Part of King Henry IV*, The New Cambridge Shakespeare, 2nd edition, Cambridge University Press, Cambridge.

Films

Chimes at Midnight 1965, dir. Orson Welles, UK. Starring Orson Welles, John Gielgud and Keith Baxter – draws from several plays, including *1 Henry IV*.

Henry IV, Part 1 1979, dir. David Giles, UK, BBC. Starring Anthony Quayle and Tim Pigott-Smith.

My Own Private Idaho 1991, dir. Gus Van Sant, USA. Starring River Phoenix and Keanu Reeves – despite the modern setting, scenes draw from the tavern scenes of *1 Henry IV*.

Website

http://internetshakespeare.uvic.ca/Foyer/plays/1H4.html – an internet edition of the play